3200703
GW01279557

THE HIT FACTORY

THE HIT FACTORY

The Stock Aitken Waterman Story

MIKE STOCK

OXFORDSHIRE COUNTY COUNCIL	
3200703041	
Cypher	25.10.04
786.94 STO	£14.99
25.10.04	

NEW HOLLAND

First published in 2004 by New Holland Publishers (UK) Ltd
London • Cape Town • Sydney • Auckland

www.newhollandpublishers.com

Garfield House, 86–88 Edgware Road, London W2 2EA, United Kingdom

80 McKenzie Street, Cape Town 8001, South Africa

14 Aquatic Drive, Frenchs Forest, NSW 2086, Australia

218 Lake Road, Northcote, Auckland, New Zealand

10 9 8 7 6 5 4 3 2 1

Copyright © 2004 in text: Mike Stock
Copyright © 2004 in photographs: Mike Stock, except for those credited below.
Copyright © 2004 New Holland Publishers (UK) Ltd

All rights reserved. No part of this publication may be reproduced, stored in any retrieval system or transmitted, in any form or by any means, electronic, mechanical, photocopying, recording or otherwise, without the prior written permission of the publishers and copyright holders.

ISBN 1 84330 729 4

Reproduction by Pica Digital Pte Ltd, Singapore
Printed and bound in Malaysia by Times Offset (M) Sdn Bhd

Picture Acknowledgements:
Plate 6: ©1986 London Records Ltd; Plate 7: ©1986 PWL/SDA/David O'Dowd; Plate 8: ©1989 WEA International Inc.; Plate 9: 1986 PWL/SDA/Chris Edwick; Plate 10: ©1988 Warner Bros. Music Ltd/Paul Cox; Plate 11: ©1987 Stylus Music Ltd; Plate 12: ©1989 Fanfare Records/PWL Records/Mainartery, London/Lawrence Lawry/Paul Cox/Simon Fowler/Terry O'Neill/Orde Eliason; Plate 15: Courtesy of KBD; Plate 16: Courtesy of KBD/Darenote Ltd; Plate 21: Simon Fowler.

contents

CHILDREN OF THE REVOLUTION	6
TO HULL AND BACK	8
YOU SPIN ME ROUND	29
NEVER GONNA GIVE YOU UP	43
WE SHOULD BE SO LUCKY!	53
HITS AND MISSES	72
SVENGALIS OF POP	80
I CAN WRITE YOU A HIT!	100
BEHIND THE SCENES	116
OPERATIONS SHUT DOWN	126
SKULDUGGERY AND MAYHEM	134
DRAGGED THROUGH THE COURTS	143
IT'S ONLY POP BUT I LIKE IT	150
BETTER THE DEVIL YOU KNOW	159
POP GOES BACK TO THE FUTURE	166
DISCOGRAPHY	176
ACKNOWLEDGEMENTS	190

CHILDREN OF THE REVOLUTION

Pop music! It's an explosive force that has shaped all our lives. Elvis Presley and The Beatles set the ball rolling in the 1950s and '60s respectively, and hit records soon became our lifeblood. While our forefathers had engaged in war and politics, we were the lucky ones – we were the first generation to enjoy a pop lifestyle.

When rock'n'roll hit the world in the 1950s, youth culture was born. At first we listened and were happy to be fans and a receptive audience. Soon, however, the realization dawned – this new music was all about personal freedom. It meant opportunities and rewards for working-class kids with the talent and energy to seize the moment. All you had to do, it seemed, was grab a guitar and live out your dreams.

However, the moguls of pop needed more than teenage stars and Elvis clones if the music business was to thrive and prosper. It needed songs – the raw material of the record industry. Essentially, it was the writers who kept the discs spinning and the hits flowing. Many of my peers dreamed of becoming pop stars, but I had in mind a more satisfying and rewarding role. From as early as I can remember, my ambition was to be a pop songwriter. I wanted to create the words and music that made pop such a living, vital phenomenon.

I spent my youth as a working musician, learning my craft. It was time well spent. Eventually, I became a founder member of Stock Aitken Waterman, aka SAW, the most successful British record-producing team and songwriting partnership of all time. During our heyday in the 1980s we wrote, produced and recorded more than 100 Top 40 singles. If we'd put all these records out under one name we would have been bigger than my earliest idols, The Beatles.

At the peak of our success, songs such as I Should Be So Lucky *and* Never Gonna Give You Up *helped launch the world-famous artists Kylie Minogue and Rick Astley. As the hits poured off the production line, SAW itself became even more famous than the stars, so much so that we were dubbed the 'Svengalis of pop'. Despite such criticism, we always insisted on making records of the highest standards. I'd grown up listening to the finest popular music of the day, and I was determined to continue this tradition. I was also adamant about giving the public what they wanted in the firm belief that what they wanted was good pop music.*

Stock Aitken Waterman sold records by the millions, created new stars and changed the face of pop music. It was no wonder the rest of the music industry and pop media called us a 'Hit Factory', a label that was later taken up by Pete Waterman to promote us. Success brought fame and great personal rewards – but they came at a price. The combination of heavy publicity and media attention was a double-edged sword. Even worse, the beliefs and aspirations of young musicians and entrepreneurs like ourselves were easily damaged by the cut and thrust of the ruthless music industry. You had to learn how to fight and how to defend yourself.

Ultimately, the pressure and machinations within the industry led to the abrupt and shocking demise of SAW. I learned the true nature of the record industry – its politics and intrigues – the hard way. People are fascinated by the story of Stock Aitken Waterman. Our domination of the charts and our scores of hits have passed into legend. Whereas we were once slated as villains and usurpers, now we are lionized by many as masters of a classic genre. It's my aim here to tell how it all came together. The Hit Factory *is about a lot of fun, hard work and innocent dreams; it's about the personalities behind the scenes and the stars whose hits lit up the charts; but it's also a story about the dark side of the industry.*

I'm always writing and composing, and I'm still looking for that elusive, ultimate pop song. Now, it's time to put the recording machine on pause and set the record straight.

TO HULL AND BACK

I was a child of the 1950s, the first decade of peace after the Second World War. It was a time when the Establishment ruled over the last days of the British Empire and when the pageantry of Queen Elizabeth II's coronation rivalled any Hollywood spectacle. It was a world of conservative tradition. After the Blitz and the Battle of Britain, it was felt the British wanted a period of calm and reflection. Well, that may have been true of the older generation, but young people like myself were desperate to escape from the austerity, food rationing and overwhelming dullness of everyday life.

There was pop music of a kind: crooners, dance bands and the escapist Tin Pan Alley music were all played on the wireless. Nonetheless, when rock'n'roll burst onto the scene it created a sensation. I was never a great fan of Elvis Presley; for kids of my age, The Beatles were to be the ultimate pop idols. For me, it was the 1960s, not the 1950s, that was the decade of liberation and inspiration. In fact, the old rock'n'roll stuff bored me witless, and never thrilled me as much as a well-crafted pop song. By the time I was ten years old I'd heard those same old riffs a thousand times, and by the time I was a teenager the music of Elvis and Bill Haley & the Comets was already part of the Establishment.

I was 12 when The Beatles hit the big-time and they kick-started my interest in pop music. The Beatles' songs married energy with simple sentiments, and they sounded new and fresh. Their sound was a strange amalgamation of American rhythm and blues and European classic pop: a truly original concept. They loved Elvis Presley and Buddy Holly, but something happened between John Lennon, Paul McCartney and George Martin in the studio that produced something totally different. Their first albums and singles, such as *Love Me Do* and *Please Please Me*, were truly inspirational.

Beyond The Beatles, however, my biggest early influences came from my close-knit family. Perhaps it was their example of hard work and their ability to adapt to a changing world that helped me find my own feet later in life. I was always eager to listen and learn. The Beatles came from Merseyside and The Animals from Tyneside, whereas I'm a 'Man of Kent', an ancient title conferred upon those born east of the River Medway. Those folk from the west side of the river are Kentish Men, who unwisely failed to pay due respect to William the Conqueror when he marched through the county in 1066.

I was born in the seaside town of Margate on 3 December, 1951. My mother, Joan, had met my father, Bill, during the war. Bill had been a radio operator in the Royal Air Force, and was wounded during a mission over Norway when shrapnel from anti-aircraft guns hit him in the eye. He was sent for treatment and recuperation at Joyce Green Hospital in Dartford, where Joan was a sister. They met, and patient and nurse fell in love.

Bill was in his forties when he eventually married my mother in Bromley, Kent in 1949. He never talked much about his own childhood, but from the stories he did tell me I gleaned limited knowledge of a wayward mother, a boys' home and going to Canada as a young teenager. In Canada, Bill ran away to sea and ended up in Argentina before returning to England and becoming a radio operator in the Merchant Navy. He also had a brush with showbiz when he trod the boards and wrote songs for a variety act. He travelled around the country, playing at variety theatres and staying in boarding houses. When the Second World War broke out in 1939, Bill signed up for the RAF.

This was as much as I knew about my father's background until recently. In fact, it was while I was putting this book together during the summer of 2003 that my younger brother Mark made a shocking discovery: my father had been married previously and I have half-brothers and half-sisters. My mother and father hadn't married until after my older brother had been born.

We discovered more details about our father's early life, too. We learned that my father's real name was not William Ralph Stock but Walter Ralph Stock. He was born in West Ham, east London on 11 October 1911 and lived with his mother Henrietta in Loughton, Essex. His father, the real William Stock, was a young labourer who abandoned his son in 1920.

As a result of his mother's 'delicate' condition, my father's two sisters used to take it in turns to look after her, do the housework and also look after my father and his two brothers. The younger brother, John, drowned in a canal in 1912 at the age of 11. Eventually my father, at the age of 12, and his older brother were sent to a boys' home called Fegan's in Stony Stratford, Buckinghamshire. It seems that neither of his parents ever visited him at the boys' home.

Walter was devoted to his mother, but it seems his devotion was not returned. When he reached 14 she 'sold' him as an apprentice for £300 and packed him off on a boat to Canada to work as a lumberjack. It was quite common practice in those days to have your children indentured and sent abroad. It was a form of slavery and is now regarded as a scandal. Walter left for Canada on 17 April, 1926, sailing from Liverpool.

Walter couldn't stand the harsh conditions in Canada, so he ran away to sea. If he had tried to return to England straight away he would have been arrested for breaching the conditions of his apprenticeship. His mother was already being sued for the return of the money she had been paid for the absconded worker, and, since she flatly refused to repay it, Walter effectively became an outlaw. In order to re-enter England, he took his father's name, William, and thereafter he became known as 'Bill'. He arrived back home on 26 November 1927 and, surprisingly, considering all that had passed between them, went to live with his mother.

Apparently, while he was in the Merchant Navy, Bill fell into a hold and broke his arm and shoulder. This put him out of work for a while, and while he was convalescing he met a waitress at a Lyons Corner House in London. She gave him some cigarettes and a cup of tea, and they struck up a relationship. They married in 1932 and had four children. The first child, Billy, died in 1941 at the age of six after contracting diphtheria. He had fallen into dirty water in a canal, an event similar to the death of my dad's own brother. We believe that the death of his first young son badly affected Dad; perhaps he felt he was reliving the nightmare from his own childhood. Billy's death was at the height of the Blitz when Bill was away from home serving in the RAF. The couple split up and eventually divorced in 1949, after Bill had met my mother, Joan.

Mother knew all about this tragic family history, but she kept it secret. Later on, when she became ill with Alzheimer's disease, she would let slip odd remarks we didn't understand. She'd say things like, 'Dad's other family in Dartford…' It was because her defences were coming down that some of the story was beginning to creep out. She had burned all the documents so that her 'shameful' story would never be exposed – the date on the marriage certificate would have shown my brother was born out of wedlock. Nowadays, of course, nobody cares.

During the 1950s my father had visited his other children. I remember him being away a lot, but I thought that was because he was a travelling salesman. These revelations upset some members of the family. It seems Bill was trying to please two families at the same time. It was a lot to have on your plate. Whatever he did, nothing will ever change my love for my father.

By the time I was born in 1951, the war had been over for six years. Yet there was still food rationing in Britain. Life was a struggle for most working people, who didn't have much in the way of money or possessions, and there was a pervasive sense of resentment. We had 'won the war', but children still couldn't buy a packet of sweets. Dad became a salesman, and worked hard to make ends meet. He could sell any product, and was so good he started his own business. He taught me a lot about selling. Here he is on how to sell a puppy, for example: 'You say, "Keep it overnight and I'll come back for him in the morning." They'll never let the puppy go.'

My father instilled in me the idea that to be a successful salesman you had to sell yourself. Dad used to go cold-calling, knocking on doors selling the *Encyclopaedia Britannica*. I went out with him when I was young and could see it was a tough job. He'd confront people with a question.

'Don't you want your child to have an education?'

'What do you mean?'

'Well, you didn't answer our advert in the newspaper for *Encyclopaedia Britannica*.'

'I didn't see it.'

'Don't you want your son to be educated? What's wrong with you?'

When he was selling double-glazing, he'd get people to talk about their favourite football team. The chap might be an Accrington Stanley supporter who'd say, 'This year we're gonna win the Cup.' How could you tell him they didn't stand a chance? You couldn't tell a guy he was mad to think that and still expect to get a sale. And you couldn't say, 'Yeah, fantastic, they'll win', because then he'd know you were lying. The only solution was to join in the dream and say wistfully, 'Wouldn't that be good for football.' That way he'd avoid being thought a liar or causing offence.

I liked Dad's approach. He knew there was always a way of making a sale. Most of the people in the pop business today are not good salesmen. If they were on commission-only they'd starve. Partly because of his own experiences in life, my father helped me understand that it's important to do the right thing and to work hard. He started with nothing but he realized that there was always a route round a problem, if you knew where to look.

Bill died in 1978 and never saw any of the success I enjoyed in the music business. My mother died in 2002, after a 20-year decline as a victim of Alzheimer's disease.

I was one of five children. My younger sister Catherine Ann Joan was a musician and played the bassoon. She had a hit record with the theme tune for the television series *To Have And To Hold*, which was written by Catherine and her husband John Worsley. John, under the pseudonym Johnny Worth, also wrote successful pop songs, particularly for Adam Faith in the early days of British rock'n'roll. Catherine died in November 2002 after a long struggle against breast cancer. My other sister Evelyn is a barrister.

I also have two brothers, Mark Charles Stock and John Stock. Mark is a magician who has written a book about sleight of hand and close-up magic. John was trained in classical music. He went to the Guildhall School of Music aged 18 and now plays in the German National Opera orchestra where he is leader of the viola section.

We're quite a mixed bunch!

Dad pummelled the Victorian work ethic into all of us and he really did work hard. I guess we were 'aspiring lower-middle class'. In 1955, Bill had saved enough to buy a semi-detached house in Swanley, Kent, where I was brought up. I went to the local primary school, followed by the secondary modern, having failed what was then called the 11-plus examination. John and Catherine both passed and were able to go to the grammar school. Fortunately, the Labour governments of 1964–70 decided we'd all go 'comprehensive'. This meant that I got to sit 'O' levels, which I passed, and I even went on to pass 'A' levels. Much to everybody's surprise, I got such good results I was able to go to university.

During my teenage years, I developed a deep love for pop music. Despite Beatlemania, it was still quite difficult to hear pop music in the early 1960s. There was no Radio 1 or pirate radio yet, and I was too young to

To Hull and Back 13

go to nightclubs. The best place to hear the latest pop records was at the fairground. I remember hearing *Love Me Do* for the first time at the local fair; the sound of the Mop-tops came spinning off the waltzer like it was some kind of hurdy-gurdy.

As a teenager, I saw a Hollywood movie about Tin Pan Alley and the tunesmiths who could write a hit song a day. I also remember hearing the story about the man who wrote *Any Umbrellas* and sold it for a half a crown. All this sparked off my fascination with composing. I taught myself guitar and began writing songs. My siblings John and Cathy became involved in music through the grammar school they attended, but I never had a music lesson. My dad could strum a ukulele and play all the black notes on a piano, but I never had any real encouragement to study music. Perhaps it was better that I didn't – without it I'm sure I was much more driven. As a child I did sing at school in assembly and in the school and church choirs, of course, and I was always told I had a good soprano voice. Music was certainly flowing through my veins, but I still don't read or write music. I was self-taught and learned to play by ear. I can hear a record and copy the music on a guitar or a piano in a way that my brother and sister couldn't. They would have to read the music, because that's the way they were trained.

> **I NEVER HAD A MUSIC LESSON**

By the time I was 19, I had a music publishing contract. I was signed up for seven years with a Medway company called Marrow Music. I had sent some early songs to them and been offered a deal. I didn't get much of an advance and the contract led me nowhere, but I did get a reputation as a budding songwriter. I was stuck with Marrow Music until I was 26, and didn't branch out professionally until after the contract ended.

In 1969 I was still making the transition from schoolboy to student. Before

I started at Hull University I took a 'gap year'. I was 18 years old and wanted to see the world. I put a knapsack on my back, donned a pair of green Army fatigues and set off with a couple of pals. We had got as far as Holland when I met a girl and ended up staying put. I may not have seen much of the world on my 'world trip', but I had a lot of fun. For a while I worked in a pornographic cinema, sweeping up after each performance for a few guilders – not the best job in the world, I'll admit. When the money ran out I hitched a ride home, kipping in the back of lorries. Eventually, university beckoned and I set off alone on a train to Hull, clutching my duffel bag and cowering inside a greatcoat. I felt like I was heading for the frozen north.

Hull proved to be an intriguing place. It had its own telephone system and bus service and was like an independent state within the United Kingdom. I developed a lot of affection for the city, even though it was very cold in winter when the wind came in from the North Sea and blew up the estuary. Hull was still an active fishing port and you knew when the fleet was in from the smell.

My intention was to study drama and theology, but everyone studying theology in those days started out with a grounding in Latin and Greek. I had no Greek, and was clearly out of my depth. I persevered for two years then left without taking a degree. That was disappointing but I'd had a lot of good times at university, mostly playing football or guitar in a local band.

There's another reason I became fond of Hull, besides fish and football. I met my wife Bobbie there. She was a year ahead of me, studying English and drama. We fell in love and moved in together. At last I had some security. I had been living in the halls of residence and was glad to escape the poky room I shared with some great big hairy fellow. Bobbie and I rented a flat above a fish and chip shop in the centre of Hull. We didn't have much money and had to buy cheap sherry when we wanted a drink. Bobbie stayed on to get her degree and when she graduated I left with her.

While I was at university I formed a band with a chap called Anthony Minghella, an aspiring keyboard player who was in my year. Also in the band was Pete Markham on guitar – the 'hairy fellow' I shared a room with! I don't think the band even had a name, though a publicist I was interviewed by many years later made one up: The Cosmics. We weren't that kind of group. We were doing free-form jazz for the drama department so that they could choreograph modern ballet dances. We did tour a bit, and I remember going to Liverpool to perform at a college.

Anthony Minghella was a clever, intellectual fellow. Side by side we directed a double-bill at Hull as part of our drama course. Minghella did one show and I did the other. His was a tightly woven, thoughtful piece and mine was all about dropping bombs with explosions and flashing lights. Now, many years later, Anthony is a successful film director and the winner of several Academy Awards for his hit film *The English Patient* (1996). Pete Markham is also in the film industry and often works with Minghella.

But the musical venture with Tony Minghella wasn't my first band. I had played in beat groups as a kid at school. As a big fan of Paul McCartney, I had bought The Beatles songbook. I pored over the chord shapes and made my fingers bleed learning how to play the guitar, keyboards and bass. I was never really interested in showing off and playing lead guitar, I only wanted to strum along to accompany myself singing. When I put my first school band together at the tender age of 13, nobody wanted to play bass because it wasn't a fashionable instrument then. But to me bass was easy.

So I began my career emulating Paul, playing bass guitar and singing. McCartney always seemed to have remarkably broad tastes. He could sing rock'n'roll even better than John Lennon in my view, and he had a fantastic ear for melody. I understood his liking for songs with a strong narrative structure that really told a story.

My family had always listened to classical and light music, so that was in my blood. I loved the songs of Rodgers and Hammerstein, and my favourite musicals were *Carousel, South Pacific* and *Oklahoma!*. There were at least five hit songs in *Carousel* alone, including *You'll Never Walk Alone*. Somehow I knew from early on that music was going to be an important part of my life.

After university, however, I drifted into a variety of low-paid jobs, despite having toyed with the idea of becoming an actor. But even when I hit a low ebb I kept faith in my dream of doing something in the pop world. Quite what or how I still wasn't sure, although the idea of being a songwriter was always at the back of my mind.

I'd bought my first Phillips tape recorder when I was 12, on the never-never. It took six years to pay for this bulky machine at three shillings a week, but it was worth every penny. I paid for it by working as a petrol-pump attendant during my school holidays. My parents couldn't have paid for it so it was down to me to raise the money.

The recorder had a special feature called 'sound on sound', which enabled me to play guitar, bass and bongos and dub vocals over the top. This was in the days of reel-to-reel tape recorders when one piece of tape passed over the recording head, like a cassette recorder. When you recorded using 'sound on sound' you weren't keeping the voices and instruments on separate tracks, you were putting them one on top of the other. By the time you'd added drums and bass, the original sound had grown so faint you could hardly hear it. The effect was strange and ghostly. I learned to put the drums down first, very loud, and then overdub the guitars and vocals, but much quieter, so I'd end up with a reasonable balance. Of course, it was fairly unsatisfactory. Eventually tape recorders were developed with four separate tracks, which meant that at last you could record a clean vocal, bass, guitar and drum sound on each track and then mix them together. Even so, I was fascinated by early reel-to-reel tape recorders and the facility to do your own vocal harmonies, even though it was incredibly frustrating at times.

It was exciting stuff, though I would have died then for the sophisticated equipment you can buy today. All the same, it was those early tape machines with their valve amps that encouraged me to record and write songs. Later on, when I could afford to buy Revox and Akai tape machines, I learned even more about recording. But, despite the dedicated interest I was showing as a youngster, no-one ever suggested music to me as a career. Pop was still a mysterious world, to be enjoyed at a distance.

In 1975 Bobbie and I got married and moved further north, to Bury in Lancashire. I was selling double-glazing and hating every minute. While I admired the work of salesmen, this wasn't what I wanted to do for the rest of my life. One day, frustration boiled over and I decided to be proactive.

In the long hot summer of 1976, Bobbie and I sold our house in Bury and moved south to live with Bill and Joan. My parents had moved out of Swanley to Birchington in Kent, and it was there that I formulated my master plan. I promised Bobbie, my parents and myself that I could make a go of it. From then on, music was going to be 'it'! I bought an electric piano and a rhythm box with three rhythm settings: rock'n'roll, waltz and Latin. I also got a small amplifier and microphone.

> **THE BIG QUESTION REMAINED, HOWEVER: COULD I EARN ENOUGH TO LIVE ON JUST BY PLAYING MUSIC?**

All set with a guitar, piano and drum box, I reactivated my hard-sell technique. I knew I could sing and play well enough, so I rang some pubs and clubs and asked if they wanted live musical entertainment. The answer was an emphatic yes. It looked like I was in with a chance. The big question remained, however: could I earn enough to live on just by playing music?

The first gig I ever did was at Avely Working Men's Club in Essex on 25 July, 1976. I took my sister and brother-in-law along, as well as Bobbie, for moral support, and sang to the customers at Sunday lunchtime and the club paid me £25. It was goodbye double-glazing and hello showbiz! I began playing bigger pubs in London, and before long I was working eight gigs a week: one every evening and twice on Sundays. It seemed the public and the publicans liked me. I was giving them the kind of music they wanted.

I was so much in demand that I picked up several residencies, including The Clarence in London's Whitehall on Monday evenings and The Sussex, a pub in St Martin's Lane, on Tuesday evenings. I also played regularly at The Pigeons in Romford and at The Badger and The Commodore in Basildon, Essex. I was having a ball, singing cover versions of classic, quality pop songs I'd learned in my garage over the summer, such as *By The Time I Get To Phoenix*, *Answer Me*, *Theme From A Summer Place* and three hours' worth of other material. It wasn't long before I was earning up to £60 a gig.

I was out all hours and travelling miles from the coast up to London each day, but the money was pouring in. I bought a car and really got going. Some pubs and clubs were better than others and had little stages in the corner where I'd set up on my own.

Although it was satisfying work, it was lonely in a way. One night in February 1977, when I was singing away in a pub in Greenwich, a guy came up to me and said, 'Do you mind if I play along with you? I'm a guitarist.' His name was Paul Challenger. I said, 'Fine – have a go.' I sat down at the keyboards and Paul stood and played the guitar, and from that night onwards we were a duo – Mirage. As a duo I could put the fee up but not double it, so I took a drop in wages, but everyone was enjoying themselves and it was more fun than playing on your own, although I still kept many of my solo residencies. By now Bobbie and I had our own flat in Blackheath, south-east London and Bobbie was working full time as a schoolteacher. I used to cook dinner when she came home from school and then whizz off to the next gig.

The pub gigs were very basic. I didn't claim to be a great keyboard player; it was just to accompany my singing. What I learned quickly was which songs went down best. You couldn't play stuff the audience didn't like; you *had* to play popular tunes. Certainly no heavy rock. If I'd started to play the hits of Led Zeppelin it probably wouldn't have been long before the landlord had shown me the door. The customers were regular working men and women and if you drove them away with the wrong kind of sound you wouldn't get paid. The landlord only asked you back if you increased his takings, and some of the pubs were quite small. Luckily, I was singing the music I liked – my tastes coincided with those of the customers. Some audiences were tough, but I could usually win them over.

Together with Paul, however, the sound was much bigger, so we could play more working men's clubs. There weren't many mobile discos in those days and lots of pubs and clubs put on live music. We began using a Roland rhythm box, which had a lot more rhythms and made us sound like a trio. Even so, it had its limitations, and I became dissatisfied with pushing buttons to stop and start. We changed tack again and began playing guitar and standing up to sing, and before long my sister Catherine and her friend Karen Gibbs joined us and we became more of a group. Catherine played keyboards and Karen sang and played rhythm guitar. Karen later went on to write her own songs and produced the band All Saints.

Next we began to audition drummers. We got through quite a few of them as the trouble with drummers is that often they're not very good or not very disciplined. I could be a bit of a tyrant: 'You can't play loudly when we're trying to sing!' Or: 'Please don't crash that big cymbal right next to my ear.' I especially didn't like drummers who sped up or slowed down the rhythm. I had worked with an electronic rhythm box seven nights a week, so I kept good time. I hated drummers who were slack, which many were. Drummers are better now because they've learned their trade using drum machines as metronomes. We were covering well-known songs so it was important we were spot on.

A breakthrough came when I was doing my Monday-night residency at The Clarence. It was during an overlap period when I was doing both Mirage and solo gigs. I was playing on my own when an impresario called Michael Black saw me. His brother, Don Black, was famous for writing the lyrics to John Barry's theme tune for the movie *Born Free*. Michael had an office above the Whitehall Theatre, just round the corner from The Clarence. He had popped in for a drink, heard my set and decided he liked me enough to give me a booking right away to play at a beauty contest. All I had to do was play *The Girl From Ipanema* while the girls walked up and down the catwalk.

Michael was a terrific guy with a great Jewish sense of humour; he was full of funny stories. In his line of business he handled lots of ready money and one day the VAT man called at his office and told him how much he owed, which was a lot. Michael looked at the guy and said, 'Okay – how much for cash?'

Michael was a larger-than-life character who helped me a great deal, firstly by booking me into posh surroundings, away from smoky pubs. As a duo, Paul and I began to play lucrative hotel gigs. It would have been difficult for me alone to keep a crowd happy in a big hotel ballroom. Michael booked us regularly for the Inn on the Park, the Hilton, the Grosvenor House Hotel and the Dorchester in Mayfair. Mirage covered the gaps between Ray McVay's big-band spots in the massive 2000-seater ballrooms. It was Michael Black who taught us how to segue numbers. We'd set a tempo and after three minutes we'd change the song. Michael would say, 'You've gotta segue, son. You can't leave 'em standing on the floor or you've lost 'em.' That was an important

> 'YOU'VE GOTTA SEGUE, SON. YOU CAN'T LEAVE 'EM STANDING ON THE FLOOR OR YOU'VE LOST 'EM.'

To Hull and Back 21

lesson. When the public are in party mood, don't stop the music! I started putting together strings of songs all at the same tempo.

As Mirage grew from a duo into a band, Michael kept the bookings flowing. We became one of the top hotel bands and could charge £500 a night. There was a steep learning curve in knowing how to please an audience. A defining moment came when I was playing with Mirage at the Dorchester for a well-to-do Arab family. It was a birthday party for their 12-year-old son and the place was full of kids jumping around the dance floor. We were playing funky stuff and the guitar player and drummer were showing off, but we were playing for ourselves and not the audience.

After a few minutes of this, the boy's mother came up to me and said, 'Michael, for the children, please play *The Birdie Song*.'

> '**MIKE, NOW PLEASE PLAY *THE BIRDIE SONG*.**'

Now, it was too much for my band to consider playing anything as uncool as *The Birdie Song**. I said, 'No, I'm sorry, we don't do it.' She kept asking and I kept refusing. Then she shamed me totally – she put £50 at my feet and at the feet of the guitarist, the singers – everyone. Then she said, 'Mike, now please play *The Birdie Song*.'

So we played the kid's favourite tune and I gave her the money back. I said to the band, 'We're playing for their boy's birthday party and we won't play a song because it's beneath our dignity? We're here to do a job, and we shouldn't expect to get a bonus for it.' We were there to entertain. It was another important lesson: if you want to play your own stuff, fine, do it in your bedroom – don't charge people money just to indulge yourself.

*The original *Birdie Song* was a polka played by Swiss accordion player, Werner Thomas, in the early 1960s. When people began to jig around to the tune it reminded Thomas of his pet ducks and geese and he named the song 'Tchip-Tchip'. A Belgian music publisher heard it in 1971 and he added Dutch lyrics. The song was a hit all over Europe by The Electronicas. When British holidaymakers came back humming the tune, UK producer Ray Levy rushed out *The Birdie Song (Birdie Dance)* by The Tweets, which got to Number Two in 1981 and spent 20 weeks in the Top 40. *The Birdie Song* was voted the worst song of all time in a poll commissioned for internet site 'dotmusic' in 2000.

There were constant battles in the band. And it wasn't just about the choice of tunes. The drummer was always speeding up or putting in too many 'fills'. I wanted the audience to enjoy themselves, and they couldn't hum along to a drum solo. When Stock Aitken Waterman formed, my concern was always identifying our audience. Most producers try to please the music industry, not the public. When you make a record the belief is that you have to please some DJ so he will play it on his radio station; he may not know an A flat from an elephant's bum, but you have to make a record to suit him. And this is even before the public gets a chance to say whether they like the record or not.

Despite all the problems of carrying a band on the road, I was successful with my new musical career, and I'd learned how to make tough decisions quickly. Along the way I sacked several guitarists. Not Paul Challenger, though. Paul left of his own accord in 1978 and I had to find a replacement. It was the same year as my father died from a heart attack. I found myself playing yet another gig on the day he passed away in hospital.

By 1980, I had sacked the umpteenth guitarist for being drunk and disorderly on stage. Guitarists were always flighty! Keyboard players could be a bit flaky, too. One in particular joined the band and proved to be an argumentative sod. His ideal set-up was to have as many keyboards as Rick Wakeman used on stage in Yes. He wanted a Mini Moog, a Hammond organ and a Fender Rhodes – the biggest and heaviest instruments around – and we carted them up and down flights of stairs and onto stages for him.

Once in a blue moon I would call a rehearsal to revamp the band and learn a new batch of songs, but this keyboard player didn't like rehearsing. Still, we loaded his gear into the van one day and were driving through Stratford in east London to the rehearsal room when he started arguing and complaining. I said, 'Look, if you don't want to rehearse, you can get out now.' He said, 'Take me to the station.' I said, 'No, if you want to get out, get out now.' I stopped the van in the middle of Stratford Broadway and dumped his Fender Rhodes, Hammond organ and Leslie speaker cabinet on the pavement and drove off and left him.

He stood there open-mouthed – he never thought I'd do it. I have no idea how he got home, and I didn't care. He lived on the fourth floor of a block of flats in Kensington and we had always carried his equipment up and down the stairs for every gig. I guess he wanted to be Emerson, Lake and Palmer, but we weren't doing that kind of stuff – not at all. That musician had pushed me to breaking point. It was hard work running a band – back-breaking work. It was a good job I was in my twenties and fit and strong.

When Mirage played the top hotels we had to wear smart suits with bow ties, but on other nights we'd play under the name of Nightwork at rock venues, such as the Golden Lion in Fulham, Dingwalls at Camden Lock and the Bridge House in Canning Town. It was the same band, but with two names and two styles. We'd earn £500 at the hotel and £60 at the pub.

Between 1979 and 1981, we were working every night of the week. I remember a special promotion we did with Nightwork at the Green Man on Stratford High Street in June 1981. We charged £1 on the door and it seemed like we'd hit the big time. We had our own publicity material and launched our own fan club called 'Nightclub: The Official Friends of Nightwork', which was run by Karen Hopkins, one of our keenest fans. One of her press releases explained the origins of the band:

> *Nightwork was formed from the remains of a commercial band called Mirage who, for a long time, played many of the top hotel engagements, e.g. Park Lane Hotel, the Playboy Club and the Hilton Hotel. The leader Mike Stock had written many songs but found that the hotel circuit*

offered little opportunity to present self-penned numbers. Earlier this year, therefore, the band got together a short set of their own material, found a pub in which to play and were quite overcome by the exceptional reception they received from the audience.

Greatly encouraged by this, they extended the number of places they could present their own material ... The group consists of Mike Stock (bass guitar and lead vocals), Terry Neilson (drums), Steve Skinner (guitar) and Marie Clerkin (lead vocals).

Karen was very enthusiastic, but her flyers quickly became out-of-date when I had to change the line-up. It wasn't long before both Steve Skinner and Marie Clerkin left the group. Changing musicians went with the territory, but it caused endless problems. I had to sack one lead guitarist on the very night we had an important gig at the Royal Garden Hotel in Kensington. An American singer called Joanna Lee had recently joined us, and she told me she'd seen a really good guitarist who had just come off a cruise ship. His name was Matt Aitken. Joanna gave me his phone number and I asked Bobbie to contact him and arrange for him to come to the Royal Garden Hotel for 6pm to run through a few numbers.

Matt got his break with the band mainly because he owned a suit. Bobbie had told him to wear a dark suit and he turned up on time and looking smart. I asked him if he knew *Boogie Oogie Oogie*, A Taste Of Honey's big 1978 hit, which has a particular guitar section that's quite nifty. Matt got it right away. Then we played *I Will Survive* and he knew that riff too. So Matt was in. That evening he played the whole gig and that's how Matt Aitken and I first met – playing *Boogie Oogie Oogie*!

Matt was born in Coventry in 1956, but grew up in Leigh, Lancashire. He had a grammar school education and went into local government as a clerk. He loved playing guitar,

> **MATT GOT HIS BREAK WITH THE BAND MAINLY BECAUSE HE OWNED A SUIT**

though, and soon came to London to seek his fame and fortune. He joined a few bands and did gigs on cruise ships. On the ships you had to be really good because you had to play every style of music. He had a solid musical background and could cover anything. And we're also both Tottenham supporters!

It's incredible to look back at our date sheets for those days. Nightwork often played every night of the week, at pubs and clubs all over London but especially in the east, including The Rose & Crown in Hoe Street, Walthamstow, The Three Rabbits in Manor Park, The Bridge House in Canning Town and The Green Man in Stratford. It was exciting. I couldn't play disco stuff in a bow tie every night. Nightwork was our way of breaking loose. Guitar, bass and drum groups were in fashion, and our style was similar to that of the new wave band The Police.

For a while it seemed as though Nightwork might take off. However, one night at a big pub in Fulham, west London, I learned another lesson, a bitter lesson that convinced me that my future lay in the studio rather than on the road. The Golden Lion was a well-known venue where there was more chance of being spotted by A&R men than there was in the East End. We were full of optimism, sure we'd soon be 'discovered'. At least we'd be well paid for a gig packed with enthusiastic fans. However, the machinations of the business soon became apparent.

In those days, promoters insisted you 'coach in' your own audience. It seemed bizarre, but luckily we had a mailing list of fans who regularly came to hear us play the original songs I'd been writing. So on Monday, 10 August 1981 we managed to pack the Golden Lion with over 300 people. I had booked three coaches and charged fans 50p a seat for them. They were also charged £2 to get in, which meant that £600 was taken on the door. It looked like it was going to be a fantastically successful night. Then the alarm bells began ringing. I had to pay for the extra bar staff and security, and rent the PA system and lighting rig from the pub as they wouldn't let us use our own. At the end of the night, after we had filled the place and put on a great show, the pub's manager said, 'Here's your share of the take: £3.85.' It was just enough for the band to get a burger on the way home. I thought, there's something seriously wrong here, I'm not doing this right.

All rock gigs were the same – you paid for the privilege of being there. I could make a living playing at the hotels, but I began to realize there was a danger that I would end up doing that forever. Indeed, there were some well-known bands that stayed on the same circuit for years. I was on a bill with the famous bandleader Joe Loss and he was nearly 80 years old.

In 1982, Bobbie and I bought a new bungalow in Abbey Wood, south London. All riverside houses built close to the Thames flood barrier, which was being erected at Woolwich, had to be sited six foot above ground level to avoid the possibility of flooding. That meant that beneath the bungalow was a large usable space. Matt and I acquired a recording desk and built our own studio there. We also formed our own record label – Sticky Label, a terrible pun. Still, we were filling the studio with clients, and running the studio and the label was becoming ever more time-consuming. Its apparent success, and the lesson I'd been taught in the Golden Lion helped me make a big decision about Mirage and Nightwork.

The last Mirage gig we did was at the Royal Lancaster Hotel on New Year's Eve, 1983. During a break I told Matt and Terry that I wasn't going to take on any more gigs, and that I was going to go into my studio to make hit records. I knew I had to give it a try. Terry wasn't convinced and decided to keep gigging, as did our singer and keyboard player. But Matt agreed to join me. So, from January 1984, we worked exclusively in the studio. Matt virtually lived in our garage. His rusting old Ford Capri stood on my drive for years. In the end, I paid someone £20 to take it away. Matt was so broke in those days that he only had one pair of shoes for gigs and one pair of trainers with the soles flapping off. I even had to buy him a new pair of trainers once.

Sad though the break-up of the band was, it allowed Matt and me to fully concentrate on writing and recording. We tried to launch a few acts but we were naïve. Fortunately, Bobbie's teacher's income and the gig money I'd saved up gave me the luxury of not working for about a year, during which time I was convinced we'd come up with some great material and a winning idea that someone would buy. The pressure was on. For all our sakes, we had to have a hit record.

YOU SPIN ME ROUND

1984 was a fantastic year for British pop. There were so many exciting records hitting the clubs and the charts. Frankie Goes To Hollywood unleashed their sensational singles Relax *and* Two Tribes, *Wham! had a Number One hit with* Wake Me Up Before You Go Go *and George Michael crooned* Careless Whisper, *the song he'd written on the top of a bus. After 1970s punk rock, pop music was back and revitalized. The public was hungry for new sounds and artists were desperate for songs.*

Matt and I were ready for action as we faced the challenges and golden opportunities of the 1980s – all we needed was a catalyst. The seeds of our success were already sown, and it was strange the way events conspired to bring Stock Aitken Waterman together.

In the bleak winter days of January 1984, Matt and I had a problem. How could we get our songwriting team off the ground? Someone had to have faith in us and our 'idea'. It was just a matter of finding the right person. So, what was our big idea? Well, we had come up with the scheme of launching a female version of Frankie Goes To Hollywood. Why not? Someone had to do it! Matt and I would write the song and then go into the studio with the two girl singers who were prepared to front our brilliant concept.

We wrote the song, *The Upstroke*, in early January, and arranged three meetings in London for 15 January. It turned out to be a momentous day. Matt and I arrived in central London with nothing more than our train fares in our pockets. We didn't even have enough money for a cab or tube, so we walked from Charing Cross to the various record company offices. One of them was in Camden Town, a mile's hike away from the West End.

Matt and I arrived in central London with nothing more than our train fares in our pockets

First, we took the idea to Rak, which was the late Mickie Most's label. However, our appointment with their A&R man was cancelled – he was sick from having had too much to drink the night before. Then we tried Red Bus, another indie label, but they blew hot and cold about the idea. Then we went to see Pete Waterman.

I'd already had some dealings with Pete a couple of years before when my brother and I had written a song – *One Nine For A Lady Breaker* – for a citizen band (CB) radio club at a time when the use of CB radio was still illegal in England. I had recorded the song in 1982 under the pseudonym Chris Britton, and it was produced by Peter Collins, the record producer for Musical Youth and Nik Kershaw. The song got a few local radio plays and found its way to Pete Waterman, a go-ahead guy who managed Peter Collins. It was because of this tenuous link that I decided to approach Pete Waterman now.

Pete was born in Coventry in 1947 into a poor working-class family. It's been said that he was illiterate until his forties. He'd certainly had a tough upbringing, and he had his own plain-speaking, no-nonsense approach to life. He worked on the railways and the mines and was apparently a union shop steward at the age of 19. He'd also worked as a Northern Soul DJ and knew everything there was to know about American disco and club music. In the 1960s he had been a jazz and R&B club DJ and compère and had supplied imported American records to everyone from The Beatles to Fleetwood Mac. He later became house DJ for the Mecca Group and by the 1970s he was a promotions man and A&R consultant for record companies, including Elton John's Rocket Records. In 1979 Pete set up his own company, Loose Ends, and in 1982 he signed Musical Youth and Nik Kershaw. To say the least, this was an impressive curriculum vitae.

We met Pete in the afternoon at his office in the Stiff Records building. We were in luck. Pete had just fallen out with Peter Collins and didn't have anybody to work with. Just as we came along he was looking around for a new kind of partnership.

We had explained our idea and how it would all work to each label. The guy at Red Bus had said, 'I'd love to see the band, where are they gigging?' He didn't understand we had invented the concept of a studio 'group'. They didn't gig! Matt and I were 'the band'. When we explained this idea to Pete he understood it right away. 'Okay, so you're the band, you make the record and the girls front it. I understand what you're getting at. I like it. Let's go in the studio and do it!'

Meeting Pete Waterman was a blessed relief. He immediately saw the potential of our plan and didn't ask stupid questions. He wanted to meet the girls who were going to front our new act, Agents Aren't Aeroplanes. The name was a quote from John Le Carré's novel *The Spy Who Came In From The Cold*. It was just a phrase, like 'Frankie Goes To Hollywood'. What did it mean? Nothing! It just had a nice sound.

On 14 February 1984 we went to the old Marquee Studio in Wardour Street, Soho. We made our track and it caused a bit of a minor stir. Barry Evangeli, a Greek Cypriot who ran a label called Proto Records with his partner Nick East, agreed to put the record on his label and it was distributed by RCA. *The Upstroke* only got to Number 60 in the charts, but it did very well in the gay clubs. This was good news because by this time the gay clubs and discos were where new acts and records were being discovered. The gay community had become a powerful force. Our records proved so popular with this group that some people thought that Matt and I must be gay.

Our idea was to make a dance record that would suit what was then called 'Boy's Town' music and later became known as High Energy or Hi-NRG. We knew exactly what audience we were aiming at. *The Upstroke* was Number One in the London clubs and quite a few different mixes of the song went around. The production team was clearly working well.

While Pete was soon to become an ally and a mentor, other characters also played a role in building what was to become SAW. In late 1983, one of the customers at our home studio was a Greek Cypriot called Andy Paul, who desperately needed a song to enter into the forthcoming Eurovision Song Contest. He asked me to write one for him and I obliged, but according to the contest rules Andy had to say he'd written it. The song, *Anna Marie Elena*, was voted for by the public and became the official entry for Cyprus in the 1984 competition.

We recorded the song for Andy and that became the second project we did with Pete Waterman. By the time we'd put out the Agents Aren't Aeroplanes record in the spring of 1984, it was time for the Eurovision contest. Pete helped me organize an orchestra to make the record and he flew out to Malta to see the contest and enjoy a jaunt with Andy Paul. *Anna Marie Elena* was a simplistic ditty, and it came ninth. It was never going to win, but Greece gave it maximum points, as you might expect.

It was decided to release the song for the Greek community in England. We went back to Barry Evangeli and Proto Records and Barry decided to put the record out himself. Intriguingly, Barry had connections with the artists Hazell Dean and Divine, and he approached us to work on a song for Divine.

When I first met Divine he wore a polo-neck sweater and looked like somebody's uncle. But on stage he would dress up in a blond wig and a frock. He had appeared in the films *Shampoo* and *Lust In The Dust* and was a bit of a folk hero on the club scene. When we recorded *You Think You're A Man* I got him to sing it well; he was a wow at the microphone. But when the record company man heard the song he said, 'You'll have to re-do it because you've got him to sound too good. I want him to

> **'YOU'LL HAVE TO RE-DO IT BECAUSE YOU'VE GOT HIM TO SOUND TOO GOOD.'**

ABOVE: *In 1977 I teamed up with Paul Challenger to form Mirage. We were in great demand at the top London hotels, where we played the dance, rock and pop hits of the day.*

ABOVE: Fashionistas! Mirage grew into a bigger band with my sister Catherine (left) singing alongside Marcus Godwin (top), Paul Challenger (top right), myself (bottom centre) and Karen Gibbs (bottom right).

LEFT: Mirage led a double life as Nightwork, a funkier outfit that performed my original songs. We escaped the posh hotels and headed for the rock circuit. (Left to right) Steve Skinner (guitar), myself (guitar, vocals) and Marie Clerkin (vocals) with Terry Neilson (drums) at a London club gig in 1979.

ABOVE: *Larger-than-life transvestite Divine was one of our first clients. We produced his/her hit* You Think You're A Man *in 1984. Here, Divine is given comfort and advice by Matt Aitken and myself.*

ABOVE: *In the heyday of SAW, Pete, myself and Matt regularly met up to talk shop and celebrate our latest hit over a drink in the nearest pub. Here we are in chart-busting mood at The Gladstone Arms in The Borough in the summer of 1987.*

ABOVE: *Bananarama – Siobhan, Keren and Sara (left to right) – were keen to work with SAW after hearing Dead or Alive's* You Spin Me Round (Like A Record). *They ended up having a string of international hits with us, including a US Number One single and two hit albums.*

growl. That growling voice is why people like him.' Divine was already in a taxi on his way to Heathrow by that time, but we managed to stop him at the airport and get him back to the studio, just so he could sing it badly. *You Think You're A Man* went out on Proto Records, who had a deal through RCA. It was very camp and gay, but it went into the charts at Number 17 in July 1984 and was our first big smash.

Divine introduced us to the world of BBC's *Top Of The Pops*. The Radio 1 disc jockey Peter Powell was the presenter, and the producers were worried that Divine was going to do something outrageous on set. They were relieved when he just stood there and wiggled about.

Hazell Dean had already had a Top Ten hit with *Searchin'* in 1983, and she was looking for a follow-up. Matt and I had written a song that Matt thought was perfect for Hazell. Barry Evangeli was on his way to Europe to see Divine in concert when Matt decided to stop him at the airport and give him the cassette. (In retrospect, it looks like there was a lot more running around at airports than music-making going on!) Matt's endeavours were unknown to Pete, but Barry liked the song and put us together with Hazell Dean and we ended up producing *Whatever I Do (Wherever I Go)*. The song reached Number Four in August 1984 and stayed in the charts for 11 weeks.

Hazell Dean was born in Essex and she had a big powerful Hi-NRG voice. She had started her singing career as a teenager when she recorded a cover of *Our Day Will Come* for Decca, which was a club hit in the late 1970s. She was then persuaded to record *Searchin' (I Gotta Find A Man)*, which got to Number Six in the UK and paved the way for *Whatever I Do (Wherever I Go)* with us in 1984.

That song we did with Hazell had a curious forerunner. It involved a visiting American singer. Before we teamed up with Pete Waterman, Matt and I were working out of our Abbey Wood studio and somehow this guy got in touch with us. He was gay so we wrote a song for him that had a camp tune and outrageous lyrics. Matt and I looked at each other and grinned. We were sure we wouldn't get away with it. It had dramatic lines like 'As the rain sweeps through the city streets' and a tune that was derivative. The American was an amateur, really, and didn't have a singing voice. In fact, when it came to recording the song, he could only speak. So he ended up talking through the lyrics but, surprisingly enough, it worked out quite well. He went off happily with his tape and we didn't hear or think any more about it.

When we began working with Pete, Hazell Dean urgently needed a song. That's when Matt tripped off to the airport to hand over the tape of the song we'd done for the American to Barry Evangeli. We had changed the lyrics, of course, but it was virtually the same tune and when it received some radio play I got a call from an irate American.

He ranted and raved down the phone. 'I am lying in my hospital bed and I turn on the radio and hear this fucking song and it's my song and… and… this woman is singing *my* song!'

'Why are you in hospital?' I asked.

'It's a long story, but I was fooling around with a jar of pickles …'

I couldn't take much more than that – he had such an affected voice and I couldn't imagine *what* he'd been doing with the pickles that had landed him in hospital. Nevertheless, I managed to apologize to him and explain. We had recorded the song with somebody else. It wasn't his song. He hadn't understood that it was our copyright and we could do whatever we wanted with it. It had become *Whatever I Do (Wherever I Go)* and was SAW's all-important first Top Ten hit – all thanks to the man with the pickle jar!

I had warmed to Pete immediately, and I liked his salesmanship. I recognized in him a man who was good at selling himself. And since that was the case, he could also sell us to the music industry. It's not ignominious to be a salesman. It's an art and a skill. I always saw Pete as a salesman and I told him so on a number of occasions. He somehow thought I was insulting him, but I wasn't. My dad was a salesman and I was proud of him. Pete had left school at a very young age and had had to bluff his way through the world, an experience that gave him a vital inner strength and a kind of aggression. He was a larger-than-life character, and he had faith in us. For the next few action-packed years our lives were to become inextricably entwined.

With both Hazell Dean and Divine we had done all the pre-production in my studio, and at that point our relationship with Pete was still somewhat tentative. He was acting like our manager, but we were more proactive in getting assignments. I didn't need a manager; I knew what time to get up every morning. I could make the arrangements in my life and I was keen to forge my own career.

Matt and I realized early on that Pete's strength lay in his vast wealth of contacts throughout the music industry. I'd come up through the gigging musicians' route, so I knew about bands and promoters. But the recording industry, A&R men and recording budgets was Pete's department. He could see there was terrific energy developing in the studio and realized the project could work. It has to be said that Pete wasn't really a musician, but he had the contacts and the energy to promote the music. Matt and I went into the studio and we made the records. We were the instrumentalists, the arrangers and producers. And even though Pete would share the credits, Matt and I wrote the songs. There was no real role for Pete in the studio; he was out and about doing the business side of things. In fact, he hardly ever came into the studio during working hours, and he'd normally come in at the end of the mix at the end of the day. Pete's role was to keep supplying us with work and putting us in touch with artists.

As that process evolved, we became the world-famous team of Stock Aitken Waterman. Our aim was to produce uplifting, working-class dance music and the slogan became 'PWL – The Sound Of A Bright Young Britain'. Success came so quickly we hardly had time to smell the roses.

'PWL – THE SOUND OF A BRIGHT YOUNG BRITAIN'

By September 1984 we seemed to have had a pretty good year. We'd done the records with Divine and Hazell Dean and we were raring to go. The bowstring had been drawn back and the arrow was in place. We only needed to let go to hit the target. I was really fired up. All sorts of people, including publishers and managers, were approaching Matt and me. Tom Watkins who managed the Pet Shop Boys wanted us to work for him. He was going to provide us with a studio and he tried to poach us from Pete Waterman. But I thought we were doing well as a team.

However, even at this early stage there were signs of tension. Initially, Pete wanted to be known as the producer of all the records. Matt and I were to be the 'directors'. It would be like the film industry: creative people direct and financiers produce. I didn't like the idea. There was no tradition in the music industry for a director. We were really the producers, although on the first records it did say 'Produced by Waterman and directed by Stock/Aitken'. I didn't like that because it gave Pete a licence to have many more 'directors' under his wing. What we really needed was to be centred and focused.

SAW came together as a team mainly because I wanted to tie Pete down. I wanted him to concentrate on us, rather than manage lots of other producers and writers. I came up with a deal whereby Pete would share everything with us, including the credits and the royalties. If he would be 100 per cent behind us, we'd split everything three ways.

After a lot of wrangling, in the autumn of 1984 we decided to dump the 'director/producer' business. I wrote the songs, Matt and I produced the records, and Pete promoted and sold them. Regardless of this we became Stock Aitken Waterman – equal partners and without titles.

By this time we were well on our way to our first Number One hit: *You Spin Me Round (Like A Record)*, which was recorded by Dead Or Alive in 1984 and released on the Epic label. Pete Burns, the lead singer of Dead Or Alive, had heard the Hazell Dean and Divine records on the radio. He made some enquiries and ended up asking us to work on Dead Or Alive's forthcoming project with CBS. They'd had one hit but were yet to come up with anything else. They played *You Spin Me Round* to Pete Waterman and he played it to us. We all thought it could be a hit. The song didn't need rewriting, but it needed a Hi-NRG production and a new arrangement. It took until January the following year for the final version of *You Spin Me Round* to be released and it took until March to get to Number One.

Then the phones mysteriously stopped ringing. I was tied up in the studio and not going out looking for work. Yet all the connections we had made seemed to amount to nothing. It was partly because people thought we'd be too busy to speak to them. They also thought we'd be too expensive. I told Pete, 'Keep us working!'.

In 1984 we'd been using the Marquee Studios, but the equipment was old and breaking down. I proposed building our own, new studio. Pete didn't like the idea at first and only agreed after lots of persuasion. Matt and I knew of some available premises at the Vineyard, in The Borough, Southwark. Pete went over and rented the space, and we started to build the studio in January 1985.

From then on the Vineyard became home. It was where we did most of our work. Now we were forming our own 'Hit Factory'. ITV's *Spitting Image* later parodied us with a conveyor belt churning out stars and, although satirical, this certainly illustrated the impact we made on the 1980s. Later on, Pete with our then managing director David Howells fostered the term Hit Factory, even though it caused controversy with CBS who already used it for its offices in New York and London.

By March 1985, the studio in Southwark was almost fully operational. We were all fired up and ready to go, but still nobody was ringing us. We pulled in an act we weren't that keen on called Brilliant, who were signed to Warner Bros. One of the backing singers I used on the Brilliant project was a girl called Desirée Heslop, and I loved her voice. Matt and I were back working at my house in Abbey Wood at this point as there was still some work going on in The Borough studio, and there we wrote some fresh songs, including *Say I'm Your Number One*. I thought it would be fine for Desirée.

After I finished recording Brilliant for Warner at The Borough, I asked Desirée to stay behind and we put down this song. Pete was on holiday. When he came back we played it to him and he absolutely loved it. She was a black singer and there were not many authentic British soul artists around. Desirée took the stage name of Princess and Pete touted the song to a few record companies. Nobody could see its potential, so we decided to put it out ourselves. As it happened Barry Evangeli and Nick East of Proto Records had had a falling out, so we took Nick East on board and at our behest he set up a new label, Supreme Records. I suggested to Pete that on subsequent records Stock Aitken Waterman should also share the publishing credits.

The deal was simple enough. We would split three ways. Pete would bear the 20 per cent administration costs of publishing out of his third. So that way Waterman would get 10 per cent and Matt and I would get a third each. We all agreed to share in that way. So now we really were a team, with the producer credit, the royalty and now the publishing. Everything we did was for our mutual benefit.

> **THE DEAL WAS SIMPLE ENOUGH. WE WOULD SPLIT THREE WAYS.**

The Princess record became a big hit in the summer of 1985 and, being the first British black soul hit, it was a watershed in British pop. It was totally different from our previous records. Thus far we had been associated with Hi-NRG pop records. This was the complete opposite. The record also solidified Stock Aitken Waterman. Until then, our association had been getting pretty shaky. After this early success, it was clear that the way forward was to concentrate on producing home-grown songs and developing both new and established talent.

At the end of 1985 Bananarama approached us. They loved the Dead Or Alive record. Bananarama had enjoyed a number of hits but were now stagnating. Their label, London Records, confirmed that the group had liked *You Spin Me Round*, and arranged a meeting between SAW and the feisty three in their tutus and Doc Martens: Sara Dallin, Keren Woodward and Siobhan Fahey. The girls were great singers and wanted to do a cover of a song called *Venus,* which was originally recorded by Shocking Blue in 1968.

Although I was pushing our own material I agreed to produce the song, and it was the starting point of a relationship in which we were not yet quite powerful enough to insist on doing our own songs. We recorded their vocals very quickly because they sang the song live in about ten minutes. It was like a honeymoon for them, as previously they had spent hours of nail-grinding torture with their old producer trying to get good vocals together. Because they knew the song already, they just breezed through it in the studio. *Venus* was a big hit in the UK and even reached Number One in America in July 1986.

These scruffy London girls suddenly became glamorous international pop divas, and I had to fly out to Miami to record their follow-up. *I Heard A Rumour, I Want you Back, Love in the First Degree* were all hits, and *I Heard A Rumour* even got to Number Four in the States in August 1987. Bananarama originated 'girl power' long before the Spice Girls came on the scene. But there was another powerful 'girlie' act on the way, too.

Early in 1986 SAW got a call from Nick East who wanted us to work with a new act called Mel & Kim. Mel and Kim Appleby were from Hackney, in east London. Mel had worked as a model and been introduced to faces in the music biz. When Nick East and their manager Alan Whitehead

You Spin Me Round 39

brought them to us, they had tremendous energy and enthusiasm. Unlike Bananarama, they had no previous hits, so we could put the whole pop project together from the beginning on the basis that we wrote and produced. Mel and Kim were very talented, but they were totally inexperienced and couldn't sing with headphones on. We had to re-organize the entire studio just so they could sing with loudspeakers as monitors instead!

First we produced a record with them called *System*, but when we went to the pub to celebrate afterwards they shocked us with their loud, crude East End girl behaviour and we quickly realized that the soul songs we had in mind weren't going to be suitable. We went back to the studio, scrapped everything and started again. We did something quite new with Mel & Kim. We used Chicago house music, which was just coming to the fore in America. It had started at the Chicago Warehouse and was being played by the resident DJs. Pete Tong, the A&R man from London Records – now the famous broadcaster and DJ – brought me a cassette of the latest US music. He'd hoped we'd use it with Bananarama, but it actually inspired our first records with Mel & Kim.

We produced four classic singles with Mel & Kim. Their songs were camp and bitchy gems with attitude, usually about crap boyfriends, shopping for clothes, dancing and having a girls' night out. *Showing Out (Get Fresh At The Weekend)* got to Number Three in the UK at the end of 1986. I sang the middle eight on that one, just because it was getting late and everyone else had gone down the pub.

Their next song, *Respectable*, reached Number One in May 1987. The video, directed by Simon West – who went on to direct the blockbuster movies *Con Air* and *Lara Croft: Tomb Raider* – won the Best Video award at the Montreux Festival in 1987, and the record itself spent 15 weeks in the charts.

These songs had a special flavour and feel, which soon became known over here as house. Matt and I had taken elements of the sound from Chicago house, including the busy hi-hat and bass drum rhythms. We added a rolling bass unlike the usual Hi-NRG bass sound. *Showing Out* was one of the first singles on which the voices sounded disembodied. We were using a French sampling machine called a Publison, which gave us 15 seconds of sampling time and enabled us to break up some of the words – '*Sho-sho-showin' out*'. It all sounded satanic, like a bad dream, and I guess a lot of the Chicago house style was drug-induced, whereas we were just trying to be experimental.

Mel & Kim's songs about clubbing and having fun turned them into sassy, streetwise pop stars who appealed strongly to the upwardly mobile 1980s generation. As they boldly proclaimed to the world: '*Take or leave us, only please believe us, we ain't ever gonna be respectable.*'

Tragically, in the middle of 1987 at the age of 21, Mel Appleby was diagnosed with cancer. She had been ill as a teenager but it was a sad time and a shocking blow when she died on 18 January 1990. Kim later started making pop records again and bravely revived her career. I have fond memories of Mel & Kim – they were sparkling rays of light dancing around the studio.

By the end of 1985, we were solid. Stock Aitken Waterman had earned around £60,000, not exactly a fortune but better than anything we'd earned before. The real money didn't start to come in until 1987, when the hits started happening overseas as well. Nevertheless, Bobbie, our son Matthew and I were able to move from the house in Abbey Wood to a bigger piece of real estate in Bexley, Kent. The Stock family were moving up in the world, and there was no threat of me having to go back to selling double-glazing or playing on the pub circuit.

There were no longer any problems finding work as artists, managers and A&R men beat a path to our studio door. Yet the sudden rush of work and the wonderful sound of ringing phones brought problems, and we soon realized that SAW needed a proper infrastructure. In February 1986 we brought in Lucy Anderson to run our burgeoning publishing company. David Howells, a man who had great experience in the record business and who was well known to the music industry, particularly after his Number One hit *Barbados* with Typically Tropical, came on board to take charge of business affairs. We needed people to cope with the cascade of contracts.

We had four staff, including Lucy Anderson, working out of a tiny room. Lucy was in a section that was six foot long by four foot wide with a sliding door. She had a desk and a computer, and all the songs we'd written were meticulously filed on shelves. Amazingly, Lucy is still working with me. The other staff were Nicki L'Amy, Sheri Revell and Sharon McPhilemy. They were all part of the team. We pulled together and it worked brilliantly. The girls were in charge of publishing, overseas licences, television and radio promotion, videos and posters and a host of administrative tasks, and they all worked in this one small room next to the studio.

Now we had office staff we began to feel like a real music biz company. Matt and I concentrated entirely on delivering records, while Pete brought in the talent and made sure we were fed with work. He didn't have to look far – talent was starting to walk in the door.

NEVER GONNA GIVE YOU UP

Rick Astley was one of SAW's major discoveries, and he became a star partly thanks to Pete's girlfriend of the time, Gaynor. She had seen him singing and was so impressed that she encouraged Pete to go and see him too. Later we asked her why she thought his voice was so good. She said, 'It makes me go all funny.' It made her wobbly! That was good enough for us.

Richard Paul Astley was born on 6 February 1966 and grew up in Newton-le-Willows, Lancashire. He sang in the church choir as a child and learned to play piano and drums. He formed his first group, Give Way, in 1981 but worked as a van driver when he left school. He then began singing and writing songs with local group FBI. Although they played rock, Rick preferred listening to American soul singers, such as Luther Vandross and Michael MacDonald. Pete went to see Rick when he was singing with FBI at a club in Warrington in 1985. He, like Gaynor, was impressed, and invited Rick to come and work in the studio with a view to making a record – without the group. So Rick left FBI behind and came to London.

Legend has it that Rick Astley began his career as a tape operator in our studio. For a time Rick did work as a studio assistant, but he was never actually a tape operator. Tape operators (or tape ops, as they were often known) were really tea boys and messengers who went off to get the sandwiches. And yes, for a year Rick did that vitally important job for us.

When Rick sang for me in the studio neither Matt nor I were certain about his voice. There was something unusual about it. Sure, he had a BIG voice, but it was either on or off. It was always at full volume and there was no subtlety. Matt wasn't convinced by it. Rick sang in tune, but we wondered whether it was really an *attractive* voice. That's when we asked Gaynor and she told us about the wobble effect. Ever since my experience at the Dorchester, when I'd refused to play *The Birdie Song*, I had known that my job was to provide the public with what they wanted.

So we made a couple of records with Rick, but they didn't work. Pete wanted to do a Motown cover, so the first song Rick did was The Temptations' 1966 hit *Ain't Too Proud To Beg*. I thought we should have done one of our own songs. The true 'boy next door' appeal of Rick had yet to emerge.

Apart from a tantrum or two, life at the studio became routine. We could have been city gents commuting to work – except there were no long lunch breaks. We had a set routine that went on for years. On a typical day in the studio we didn't stop working. I'd arrive at 11am and the tape op – who could have been Rick – would make us a cup of tea.

If I was writing a song for a particular artist, I'd ask him or her to come in around lunchtime. It's not fair to ask people to sing in the morning; it's not good for the voice. So from 11am to 1pm I'd be writing a song, with Matt sitting over the keyboard or drum machine. I'd already be armed with an idea. I'd probably have woken up with a song in my head and thought about it in the bath. Then, as I drove from my home in Bexley along the A2 and through the streets of London, I'd have been thinking about the song I had to write that morning.

One morning in November 1986 I found Pete talking to Ian, one of our keyboard programmers. Pete was saying, 'I've got this great idea for a song for Rick!' But he couldn't get Ian to understand what he meant. I put down some chords I thought might complement Pete's idea. He had the title *Never Gonna Give You Up*, although Pete says that Rick Astley came up with it in conversation. Pete had been talking about his girlfriend and Rick had said something like, 'You're never gonna give her up, are you?' They both thought it was a good title for a song. So Pete had come in with the title and tried to convey the idea to the keyboard player. That was one of the few times Pete instigated a song, and it wasn't even that original – it was also the title of a B-side from a Musical Youth record he'd made with Pete Collins a few years earlier, plus there's also a Barry White song called *Never, Never Gonna Give Ya Up*.

Anyway, I took it from there. I had to sort out the tune and the lyrics and tried to come up with something appropriate. Rick, who was only 19, told us he'd had a girlfriend since he was a kid in junior school – they'd grown up together. I thought the title 'Never Gonna Give You Up' made a nice story of life-long fidelity. I started working on the verse, and the lyrics were based on what I knew about Rick's relationship with his girlfriend. When I finished writing the song I remember sitting next to the engineer Mark McGuire and singing:

Never gonna give you up
Never gonna let you down
Never gonna run around and desert you
Never gonna make you cry
Never gonna say goodbye

Then I was stuck for a line, although I knew I wanted it to rhyme with 'cry' and 'goodbye'. Mark suggested 'tell a lie'. So it became '*Never gonna tell a lie and hurt you*'. So I owe Mark £30 for the line at £10 a word! Finally, we got Rick to sing it over a basic rhythm track but with nothing much else.

Matt and I spent weeks and weeks on the accompaniment to *Never Gonna Give You Up* – the longest we had ever spent on any track. We drove ourselves barmy working on that record. I would go to bed with a tape loop buzzing around my head after 12 hours in

> **WE DROVE OURSELVES BARMY WORKING ON THAT RECORD**

the studio. It was torturous, even though working out the right tempo for the song wasn't rocket science. Some psychologist has probably done a thesis on this, but we worked out that the average resting heart works at 60 to 80 beats per minute, so we always made our songs twice the resting heartbeat with the intention of generating excitement and getting the feet tapping.

Our Hi-NRG songs were being played at around 130 beats per minute. Today's dance stuff is faster still, but perhaps their danceability can be put down to the substances many of today's clubbers take. Most of our big pop dance hits were 120 beats. Strangely enough, the hit we eventually had with Rick Astley was played at 114 beats per minute.

We tried out different grooves because it had to be danceable, accessible and radio friendly. We hunted for bass lines that would dictate the flavour of the track. In the end we hit upon the idea of adapting the bass line rhythm from a 1985 Colonel Abram song called *Trapped*. Colonel Abram only had this one hit, but the song had a great bass line! We took the basis of the rhythm, which was very syncopated, and it seemed to do the trick.

We played it to Pete but didn't get much of a reaction, so we put it aside. I got the occasional phone call from our MD Dave Howells because Rick at that time was signed in principle to RCA and they kept demanding to know when his first single would be ready. We kept saying, 'Not quite yet.'

Six months later, in spring 1987, I was walking up the stairs when I heard the record being played in one of the offices. I met Pete at the top of the stairs and we both said, 'That sounds good. Who is it? My God, it's Rick!' We then called RCA. 'This is a smash hit, get on with it.' And it was. Rick Astley's debut single was released in July and topped the UK charts for five weeks. It also topped the charts in 16 other countries and was the biggest-selling single in the UK in 1987. Then it went to Number One in America in January 1988, where it stayed for two weeks.

Never Gonna Give You Up was a big record for us, even though our first Number One in the States had been with Bananarama. I felt vindicated in my discomfort with doing 'covers' for Rick – he had an unusual voice and

I wanted to make the most of it. The covers we did record in the early days only ever made it on to the second album. I dug my heels in over Rick doing original songs and that was what helped launch 'the boy next door' to become one of the biggest stars of the late 1980s.

Considering the hours of work that went into that one song, it was kind of funny that we should later be sued by a woman who claimed that Rick Astley had stolen the song from her. The whole story is bizarre. The woman claimed that Rick overheard her singing the song to a friend on a bus in Hackney. She said that she had written the song for one friend and was singing it to another to see what she thought. The woman claimed to have an original recording of the song stamped by the Post Office that predated our recording. However, these original tapes just happened to be stolen from her solicitor's office and so the case was dropped. Matt and I shed blood, sweat and tears over that song, and it certainly wasn't anyone else's work!

Once in a while 'the real world' impinged on the pop world. In March 1987, there was a terrible disaster in the North Sea when a car and passenger ferry, the *Herald of Free Enterprise*, sank while leaving Zebrugge port, with the loss of many lives. It was suggested by the *Sun* newspaper that we should organize a charity record to help the appeal fund, which they would sponsor. We were conscious of the importance of this record, and we made sure we came up with a big hit that would raise lots of money for victims of the disaster.

The decision was taken to record a new version of The Beatles' classic *Let It Be* with a huge star cast of recording artists and celebrities, including Sir Paul McCartney himself. The song was recorded over the weekend of 14–16 March 1987. All sorts of artists from the 1960s, '70s and '80s came to the studio: The Drifters, Kate Bush, The Alarm, John Altman, Rick Astley, Bananarama, Boy George, Bucks Fizz, Hazell Dean, Frankie Goes

To Hollywood, Mark Knopfler, Terraplane, Kim Wilde and Princess to name a few.

We used the original 1970 tapes from Abbey Road. That was a great experience – you could hear The Beatles' producer George Martin saying 'Take 32' on the tapes as in the 1960s they used to record complete takes. Working with Paul McCartney was a big thrill too. He sang the first verse alone. We had some timing and tuning problems because we had to add drums and bass and other singers to the original recording for the rest of the verses, and as Concert 'A' on the original recording moved from 440 beats to 442 beats on modern synthesizers, we also had to cut Paul's vocal into small sections and piece it back together to achieve perfect tuning and timing; but he gave us the thumbs-up and liked what we had done.

The Zebrugge record was a particularly painful experience and was physically and mentally exhausting, both because of the tragic circumstances and because of the amount of work involved in making it. It entered the charts on 4 April 1987, spent three weeks at Number One and sold two million copies. In the process we knocked our own Mel & Kim off the Number One spot.

A few years later, Matt was on holiday in the West Indies when he read in the papers about the Hillsborough tragedy, in which 96 people, mostly Liverpool fans, were crushed to death at a football stadium in Sheffield. He was shocked, and wondered who might be doing the inevitable charity record. It turned out to be SAW – I had already started working on it while he was lying on the beach. Paul McCartney turned up for that one, too, and sang *Ferry 'Cross The Mersey* (originally a hit for Liverpudlian band Gerry and the Pacemakers in 1965). Gerry Marsden also joined in, but McCartney came and sang. Paul wanted to stay and help the process, putting on extra guitars and stuff. I couldn't get rid of him! That was absolutely fantastic for me. Paul McCartney was my all-time hero, and together we got the new versions of both *Let It Be* and *Ferry 'Cross The Mersey* to Number One. Even The Beatles hadn't done that – the original *Let It Be* only got to Number Two in March 1970.

A year later we also got involved in another important charity event, one which had surprising consequences. We went to the Variety Club of Great Britain dinner and put ourselves up as a prize at the charity auction. The highest bidder got to make a record with Stock Aitken Waterman. EMI bid and gave £50,000 to charity, and we agreed to make a record with a band they had signed called Brother Beyond. We ended up having a big hit with them called *The Harder I Try* in July 1988, which was followed up with another Top Ten hit, *He Ain't No Competition*, in the autumn, but then the boys went off to do their own thing.

By now, Stock Aitken Waterman had become a household name. We were becoming as famous as the artists. All three of us were at the forefront of the pop music scene. We were creating acts from nowhere and launching them to become major international stars. Nothing quite like it had ever been seen before. SAW was a phenomenon. As we started to get a major slice of market share, so we came to the attention of the major record labels. It was then that Pete, admittedly SAW's mouthpiece, started becoming a bit *too* vocal.

We were all proud of our success, but soon Pete began saying things that were frankly preposterous, such as calling us the saviours of the music industry. We started making enemies, and it was the start of a backlash. From the reaction in some quarters of the press you'd have thought we were child molesters or mass murderers. We were accused of creating 'cheap British DIY indie pop' and 'Thatcherite disposable chip shop Britain fodder targeted at bored teenagers in shopping centres'. Such snobbery! We were only writing simple uplifting pop tunes, but we were now so successful that we were displacing our own records from Number One. This kind of success could lead to problems. I was starting to get nervous.

But I was passionate about what we were doing, and the more the industry tried to put us down with personal and spiteful attacks, the more determined I became to prove them wrong and get my own back. The end result of all this backbiting was to be a record called *Roadblock*, which certainly got the industry talking.

> **'I HOPE YOU GET YOUR NEEDLES STUCK UP YOUR ARSES.'**

The worst moment in all the backlash came when we went to receive an award for a Bananarama dance mix at a *Disco Mix Club* ceremony at London's Royal Albert Hall in 1987. As we went up on stage all three of us got pelted – I even got a can of urine thrown over me. The audience was made up of DJs, armed with whistles and wearing funny hats, and we were anathema to them. Pete Waterman grabbed a microphone and said, 'I hope you get your needles stuck up your arses.' You had to admire his guts, but we beat a hasty retreat from the hallowed hall.

We ended up in the pub near our studio in The Borough, still wearing our best suits for what was supposed to have been a wonderful evening. Out of the blue some bloke came up to Pete in his leopard-skin-trimmed suit and joked, 'That's a nice suit, mate.' Pete was still seething about what had happened at the awards ceremony. He was so wound up that he ended up going chin to chin with the joker. Fortunately, we had Rick Astley's minder with us, who was also our driver-cum-bodyguard. He rushed over to separate the two men and prevented them from coming to blows. Pete was angry and hurt at the reception we'd received at the Royal Albert Hall. He'd been a disc jockey himself and he thought they were his people – that was the world he'd established himself in. Now it seemed they hated what we were doing. He was bitterly upset.

Apart from the pelting from the DJs, we were also getting lots of digs from the music press. *Black Echoes* was particularly hostile towards us – they would review Bananarama singles only to say how bad they were. We also got bad press from *Melody Maker*, *NME* and *Sounds*. The movers and groovers hated what we did. However, we got our own back. We found a very neat way to get our revenge on the knockers.

One week when Pete was on holiday and Matt wasn't around I went into the studio and wrote and produced a song a day, all of which turned out to be big hits. On the Friday, at a loose end, I put a rare groove track together of funky bass, a drum rhythm and a guitar lick. When Matt came back I asked him if he could think of a suitably trendy title. He said he'd heard a radio DJ announce a party that would be so well attended that there'd be a roadblock. So, I said, 'Right, we'll call the song *Roadblock.*' We chanted over the backing track and added saxophone and backing vocals until it sounded really chunky and funky. We left a copy on the desk of our promotions manager, Tilly Rutherford, who was amazed that we'd just made it up in the studio. On first hearing it he'd thought he recognized it from an original 1970s version!

I guess we were playing a trick on people. I played the whole of *Roadblock* to Siobhan of Bananarama before it was released. When I asked her what she thought of it, she said, 'Yeah, it's a 1970s funk track, isn't it? You guys could never do anything like that.' She actually said those words. I let her stew for a while. Although she thought the song was fantastic, when I finally let on that SAW had done it she wouldn't believe me. So Matt and I set up a drum pattern, got the bass guitar out and played a couple of bars. She loved it so much that Bananarama wrote a song over the top in an identical groove, called it *Mr Sleaze* and put it on the B-side of *Love In The First Degree.*

Of the three girls in Bananarama, Siobhan was the most difficult. After she split from the other two girls she went off to form Shakespeare's Sister in 1988, which I thought was a lot of appalling nonsense, and resembled a Gothic pantomime. Bananarama loved dressing up more than anything else. Siobhan had a tough exterior and she argued about the songs. I found it very difficult working with them, especially when we were forced into writing with them rather than for them. It was a recipe for disaster, because Siobhan wanted to move away from pop. As with a lot of artists, her 'mates down the pub' influenced her, helpfully offering advice on what they were doing wrong and insisting they should be doing something 'grittier'.

Pete decided to promote *Roadblock* as a club single without letting anybody know it was SAW. We had some white label vinyl dance versions pressed and Pete sat up for hours with a soldering iron burning out the mark that showed it was made in England. We stamped our New York lawyer's phone number on it, so if anybody called they'd think the disc originated from America.

We put the record out in the clubs and all the trendies loved it. People claimed they'd still got the original, yet it was something we'd just done in the studio. Then we got some press reviews. *Black Echoes* said: '*Roadblock*: the best goddamn dance record of 1987.' They had no idea it was Stock Aitken Waterman – the masters of 'manufactured pop'. We were successfully fooling the cognoscenti, those hip people in the know who had slated and hated us. We had shown that we weren't incapable of doing anything else.

> '*ROADBLOCK*: THE BEST GODDAMN DANCE RECORD OF 1987.'

The truth was I had cut my teeth on guitar rock and had played for years with bands on the road. I've got the scars to prove it. I had earned my living as a 'muso' and I understood all of that. If people didn't like our records then the answer was – 'Don't buy 'em.' But they did – in the millions.

But what is really ironic is that the critically acclaimed *Roadblock* was one of the few pop records we put out that never made it into the Top Ten.

WE SHOULD BE SO LUCKY!

By 1987 we had a sparkling roster of acts, including the debonair young Rick Astley who was already dominating the charts. We were writing songs round the clock and spending our lives in the studio. We knew instinctively what the public wanted and how to cater for our diverse artists, all of who were hungry for hits.

The words and music we wrote were invariably sparked off by the personalities of our eager clients. It may have seemed that we had created a 'factory', but the songs were handcrafted and tailor-made. There was no cold, calculating formula, as the critics sometimes claimed. Our aim was simple: to make great quality bespoke pop records.

In the process, we had become like a fighting machine, and I was raring to go. Pete had set up his own label PWL (Pete Waterman Ltd), which was always seen as our in-house label even though neither Matt nor I were directors or shareholders. Matt and I had been offered the opportunity to go in on the label, but we chose not to; I had some doubts about the label's prospects, and preferred not to take the risk. But as SAW we were all singing from the same hymn sheet. We recorded and produced our own songs and only rarely chose the easy option of doing covers. We ran a tight operation that was taking the world by storm. The first artist on PWL had been the girlfriend of former Rolling Stones bass guitarist Bill Wyman, Mandy Smith, but the next hit artist was a young Australian girl called Kylie Minogue.

Kylie was beautiful, talented, had a wonderful voice and was an exceptionally hard worker. Television had given her celebrity status as an actress and it seemed as though there was nothing she couldn't achieve. Her incredibly successful and long-lived international music career began in 1988 with five UK Top Ten smash hits. And it was all thanks to the Hit Factory. Soon she was paired with fellow Australian Jason Donovan and together the young Aussies had even more hits. Kylie and Jason were perfect superstars for the glam-conscious 1980s.

However, it's lucky that the magical partnership between SAW and Kylie ever got off the ground, as when Miss Minogue arrived in London hoping to start her UK pop career she was ignored, kept waiting and generally mistreated. It was all very unfortunate and only the most grovelling apology could heal the wounds. That, and a very catchy song that would transform her life.

●

Towards the end of 1987 I was working hard with Samantha Fox, Bananarama, Donna Summer, Rick Astley and Mel & Kim. It was frantic. Often I lost track of who was on the schedule. I'd drive into our south London studios in The Borough and say, 'Who's coming in today? Oh, Sam Fox, great!' She would be due in at 3pm. Then we had to finish with Sam to make way for Rick Astley in a sharp new suit, anxious to record, for example, *Together Forever.*

On one particularly busy day I was working with Bananarama in the morning and expecting Rick in the afternoon, when I got a call at lunchtime from a worried-sounding Australian.

'Mike – when can we come over?'

'Sorry? Who's coming over?' I said.

It was Kylie Minogue's manager, Terry Blamey. He and Kylie had been in London for ten days waiting to see us and they were due to fly back to Australia that afternoon. Kylie was booked onto a 4pm flight from Heathrow.

'We flew over here to make a record with you!' fumed Blamey.

I turned to the studio manager. 'What's all this about? Who the hell is Kylie Minogue?'

Back came the answer. She was an up-and-coming starlet who had a leading role in an Australian TV soap called *Neighbours*. 'Didn't Pete tell you?'

'No, he didn't!'

Pete was in Manchester. I grabbed the phone and called him.

'Pete. Is there something you forgot to tell us? I'll give you a clue. Kylie Minogue.'

'Oh, hell. I forgot.'

'Well, she's here now. She's just arrived downstairs in the office and she's due on a plane back home in about three hours. She's expecting to make a record with us and she's been sitting around in her hotel room for ten days waiting for our call.'

Eventually, I got some more information about the mystery girl who was now waiting downstairs in reception. Apparently she was 20, fabulous-looking, could really sing and was a big star in Australia, thanks to *Neighbours*. The soap was currently being shown in the UK on a daytime slot and was gathering cult status. The BBC had already tipped off our business manager David Howells about her and the ball was in our court to come up with a hit song.

> 'PETE. IS THERE SOMETHING YOU FORGOT TO TELL US? I'LL GIVE YOU A CLUE. KYLIE MINOGUE.'

I went down and Terry Blamey introduced me to Kylie. At first sight she didn't look like a star. She was wearing little NHS-style glasses and seemed quite ordinary. I asked her to sit down and have a cup of coffee. 'I'll be right back,' I said, going into the studio and muttering about Pete under my breath. I said to Matt, 'We're going to have to sort this out, now!' It was 1pm and we had nothing ready.

Matt and I sat down and brain-stormed. What did we know about her? We made a list of all the things that Kylie was doing. Then it occurred to

We Should Be So Lucky! 55

me. She couldn't have any time for a love life. She's such a lucky girl, she's full of talent and charm, but she hasn't any romance in her life. I thought of the old saying, 'Lucky at cards, unlucky in love.' Matt and I decided we liked the word 'lucky'. Kylie was young and had everything going for her. She should be so lucky.

I Should Be So Lucky sounds all pink and fluffy, but it's a sad little song. There is a wistful verse before she sings, 'I should be so lucky in love'. Anyway, the idea worked and I devised a tune very quickly on a keyboard. I scribbled down the lyrics and started singing the tune to Kylie. I soon realized she had a higher voice than I'd imagined and I'd pitched the tune too low, which meant her voice wasn't projecting enough. It began in the key of A with the melody starting on an E natural and ended up in all sorts of keys. There wasn't time to rewrite the song so I took a risk and simply moved the tune up to start on the note of A. Not something I would normally do, but this was an emergency. It began to flow. I sat with my fingers on the keyboard and worked out a suitable drum pattern. Most of our successful songs have an obvious chorus, but the verses and bridges were often quite complex to allow the song to 'grow'.

In fact, *I Should Be So Lucky* goes through a whole range of chords and movements, which makes it less contrived. Most composers write pop songs on a groove. They go, 'Here's my song' and strum a riff that goes on ad infinitum. I prefer to write songs like they used to for Broadway musicals; songs that go somewhere and reveal lots of different melodies. The media was often quick to criticize us, yet in a sense we were traditional songwriters.

I am frequently amused when I hear Pete talk on television and in the press about the creation of many of our hits as he can get a bit confused sometimes. Like the time he said that he 'nicked' Pachelbel's 'Canon' in order to write *I Should Be So Lucky*. Johann Pachelbel (1653-1706) was a German composer and organist whose works profoundly influenced J.S. Bach. Try as we might, Matt and I can find no connection between Pachelbel and our song for Kylie.

The next step on that momentous day was to get Kylie to sit on a stool in the studio and record her first ever Stock Aitken Waterman number. I sang the song to her and she sang it back at me immediately. She was so quick. Kylie was a trained performer and learned a script in a day for *Neighbours*, so remembering a lyric was quite easy for her. Oddly enough, Matt didn't like her voice; he thought it was too tremulous. But, as with Rick Astley, as soon as you heard the voice you recognized it. Nobody would say Bob Dylan is a brilliant singer, but he is certainly distinctive.

When Kylie went behind the microphone she was pitch perfect and her timing was spot on. We had the whole song written and recorded in 40 minutes. She was out of the studio before 2.15pm and on her way to the airport. We didn't know quite what we'd got on tape, but I breathed a sigh of relief. Then Rick Astley came in and for the time being we forgot all about Kylie's lightning recording session.

We only had a rough board mix down with a few instruments, including a bass, brassy synth and her vocals. A few weeks later we added some backing vocals to this and several other songs we were working on. Once we had finished working on Kylie's number we put the tape away. It was November 1987 and we had loads of other projects to put to bed. Then we got a call from her Australian label, Mushroom Records, asking what was happening with the song. We kind of bluffed because I wasn't sure we had a hit. I didn't want to commit myself, and tried to ignore the tape gathering dust in a drawer.

Then came our office Christmas party. One of the guys on hand to provide the music was a DJ known as Pitstop. Pete and I were having a drink when a song boomed out of the speakers.

'Who's this?' Pete snapped.

'It's Kylie, Pete – that girl you forgot was coming over.'

'Bloody hell – this is a smash hit!'

So it was Christmas 1987 before we realized what we'd got, and in the

New Year we moved on it. Amazingly, nobody in the industry was interested. At first we took it around the major labels, but there were no takers. There is an explanation for this bizarre non-reaction. The music industry is peopled mainly by failed musicians who like 'real music'. They don't like the kind of instant pop that appeals to the general public. Absolutely nobody was interested in a record we thought was an obvious smash. So, in February 1988, we put it out on the PWL label.

Things soon began to hot up, and there were some remarkable side effects. Our hit with Kylie gave us the sort of dominance that earned the fear and dislike of many in the music business. Yet others, such as the distributors, were delighted and even overwhelmed by our success. And one of the most important factors in gaining a big hit is record distribution – if you can't get the product to the shops in time to satisfy public demand your 'hit' will die.

Steve Mason was chairman of Pinnacle, an independent pressing and distribution company. His company was only moderately successful before we gave him the job of distributing *I Should Be So Lucky*. At first the song crept into the charts at Number 78, so we only pressed up a few thousand. Then all of a sudden the phones started ringing and shops all over the country were shrieking, 'We need more, we need more!' Steve Mason rang me, sounding stunned. He was handling orders for over 800,000 copies of the single in the UK alone. He was working night and day alongside his staff, personally picking records off the shelves and packing them, and even spent a whole weekend getting them onto lorries.

Eventually, the record broke into the Top Twenty and shot up the charts. The record nobody had wanted was now Number One and stayed there for six weeks. Kylie Minogue had become a major pop star as a result of her hit with *I Should Be So Lucky*. Soon after, *Neighbours* was on British TV every evening in a prime-time spot.

So, despite what people think, it was the record and Kylie's pop success that generated more interest in the programme, and not the other way round. Even so, *Neighbours* broke the mould and every British teenager dreamed of becoming an Australian beach boy or girl. Kylie's career went crazy. Apart from the UK, *I Should Be So Lucky* was Number One in Australia and in 25 other territories and a major success elsewhere, including countries such as Germany where they hadn't even seen *Neighbours*.

Then came the problems. People began asking what her follow-up was going to be. The truth was we didn't have any more material. Kylie had gone back to Australia and we doubted that she was planning to rush back to south London for another plastic cup of coffee in the foyer. The message came back: 'She ain't coming over and she doesn't wanna talk to you guys.' It wasn't surprising after we had treated her so shabbily in London. We could only imagine the conversation she must have had with her manager.

> **'SHE AIN'T COMING OVER AND SHE DOESN'T WANNA TALK TO YOU GUYS.'**

We had to make amends. I told Pete I would go over to Australia to see her and to try to get her to record the follow-up. I had a terrible flight: 36 hours on the plane, complete with engine problems and doors that wouldn't open. We got stuck in Bombay and then in Singapore. When I finally got to Australia I went to meet Kylie's parents at her home to apologize to her in person. After our huge success with *I Should Be So Lucky* I was quite prepared to crawl on my hands and knees and beg her to forgive us.

When I met her again she seemed incredibly relaxed about it all. Nevertheless, I'd been told she was really quite upset about what happened in London. I was straight with her and explained that we hadn't known who she was and that I'd never even seen *Neighbours*. We spent our lives in the studio and just didn't have time to watch soap operas. On top of that,

Pete hadn't told Matt and me to expect her. So I apologized profusely and suggested we try and record some more songs.

Now it was Kylie's turn to be difficult. She was busy filming *Neighbours* every single day. She could only come to the studio with me after 7pm for a couple of hours. Then she had to get home, learn a script and get up at 5am for the next day's shoot. It was a tough time for her; she was under a lot of pressure trying to juggle a pop career with TV stardom and was often tearful.

However, I somehow managed to get enough for the follow-up single, *Got To Be Certain*, and one other track that turned up later on her album. I stayed for five days, took the tape back to England, and Matt and I finished it off. *Got To Be Certain* was a song we'd written for Mandy Smith, but she couldn't cut it so we gave it to Kylie. Normally we would have written one specially for her, but she was so good and quick she could do any song easily. She was more concerned about learning her script in time for the next episode of *Neighbours*.

A lot of people had a problem with the kind of pop music we were producing with Kylie Minogue. I knew it wasn't rock'n'roll. There were no guitars on her records and it wasn't so-called 'real music'. But even if *I Should Be So Lucky* was a manufactured pop song, it still had a fresh innocence and charm that captivated people. It had a bittersweet irony that you could take on any level. I still stand by that song. Although it took only 40 minutes to write and record, it took almost 40 years' of combined experience to make it a hit.

Kylie Minogue has had to live the song down ever since. She has even been through the purging experience of reciting the lyrics aloud as poetry at the Royal Albert Hall. She found it difficult to live with because it was such a big hit. I never intended to follow it up with anything like the same sort of song. We moved Kylie from doing bubble-gum pop to becoming a much more serious artist in less than two years. During that time Kylie and

SAW had a string of 15 Top Ten hits and four Number Ones. Her singles sold in millions, and when her first album in the UK came out in August 1988 it sold 2.8 million copies.

We did four albums with Kylie in 18 months and wrote and produced almost all the songs. The only covers we did were *The Loco-motion*, originally by Little Eva, which Kylie had already had a Number One with in Australia in 1987, and *Tears On My Pillow*, a cover of a 1950s song for a feature film she was to star in called *The Delinquents*.

But there were too many people in her life and my life for us to really get to know each other. I think she regretted not spending more time in the studio. She had a busy schedule that took her all over the world. Her management would tell me: 'She's got Wednesday afternoon off'; I would have a batch of songs waiting and she would breeze through them.

It worked well and I think she thought it was easy. In fact, it wasn't easy at all; what we were doing was very difficult, but it was honed and focused. It was what went on when the artists left the studio that mattered. The real work went on behind the scenes. Matt and I were the backing band and they were the guest singers. I lost sleep and got grey hair trying to make them famous and keep their bank balances and egos inflated.

We were selling so many records that people were beginning to choke. Our artists flooded the airwaves and dominated the charts. Then SAW unleashed another pop idol who would sell records by the million and cause just as big a sensation.

It was a red-letter day in 1988 when Jason Donovan first came to Britain to record a song with us. Jason was a great pop star. The girls loved him and for kids around the world he represented a wonderful Australian lifestyle. He was young and handsome – Mr Sun, Sea and Sand. He was also a very relaxed guy and a dream to promote. But as a singer he was not one of the best. He needed a lot of help.

Jason came to London with the firm intention of launching a serious vocal career. He had already made a good start, having been involved in showbusiness since he was a kid. Jason Sean Donovan was born in Malvern, Victoria, Australia on 1 June, 1968. His father Terance was a well-known actor. Jason's parents split up when was a child and he relied on his father for guidance. He sang in a choir when he was only five years old and had piano lessons from an early age. His first television appearance as an actor was in a series called *Skyways* when he was 11. In 1985 Grundy TV auditioned him for a role in the soap *Neighbours*. Jason got the part of Scott Robinson, opposite Kylie Minogue, who was Charlene. The show enjoyed astonishing success, mostly thanks to the riveting on-screen romance between Jason and Kylie. Millions watched their relationship lead up to a screen wedding that drew record television ratings around the world.

A pop career beckoned and Jason, like Kylie, was signed to Mushroom Records in Australia. However, following Kylie's success in the UK, it was felt that Jason should also go to London to work with Stock Aitken Waterman. Everyone was confident we could provide him with smash hits.

I wasn't keen on doing a record with Jason at first. Neither were Matt or Pete. We thought it wasn't right for SAW to work with both Jason and Kylie. We assumed they were in competition with each other, though we were certainly wrong about that. Despite our misgivings, we knew it was an opportunity we wouldn't be able to resist. At first Jason worked with producer Pete Hammond, another member of the SAW organization. When he came to work with us, he recorded *Nothing Can Divide Us*, which had originally been written for Rick Astley, but Rick at that point was uncertain where he wanted to go with his career. Jason took the song and made it a great hit – it reached Number Five in the UK in September 1988 and was Number One in Japan.

After this success the next idea, born out of public demand, was that Kylie and Jason should sing a duet to coincide with the planned screen marriage of their *Neighbours* characters, Scott and Charlene. It was the biggest pressure I'd ever felt, because we thought doing a duet was going too far. I thought the public might gag on the idea. But when our business manager David Howells walked in and told us Woolworth had taken an advance order for 400,000 copies for a Christmas duet by Kylie and Jason, the brainstorming sessions started in earnest. Somebody threw out the question, 'What do they write on Christmas cards?' Promotions man Tilly Rutherford said, 'Especially for you'. It was a great title, and I knew it would be a hit. I wrote the song based on Tilly's suggestion and sang it with one of our backing singers. Matt then took the demo and went to Australia to record the vocals with Kylie and Jason. *Especially For You* shot to Number One in January 1989 after being held off the top slot over Christmas by Cliff Richard's *Mistletoe and Wine*.

Jason next returned to the SAW recording studio on 8 February 1989. We had a song ready for Australia's favourite heart-throb called *Too Many Broken Hearts*. Pete had come up with the idea for the title. Later on Pete told the press that he wrote *Too Many Broken Hearts* in ten minutes on the toilet. The truth is he only came up with the title and his version was 'There Are Too Many People Wandering Around With Broken Hearts'. Diplomatically, I suggested this might be a bit clumsy. I simplified it to *Too Many Broken Hearts*.

I don't mind Pete saying anything that makes him look big – as long as he doesn't make me look small. I felt that it took something away from me when he said things like, 'I wrote the song on the toilet.' According to Pete's logic, coming up with a title is the same as writing the song. Pete's titles were rarely any good in themselves; I would have to take the bones of them and make them work to accommodate him. The trouble is that, then and now, Pete gets away with blue murder about SAW's songs. I'd be happier to say that we all wrote the songs together. I always wanted SAW to be like a stick of rock – wherever you chopped off a piece it would say Stock Aitken Waterman all the way through.

We recorded *Too Many Broken Hearts* that day and once the session was over, Jason flew back home. By March it was Number One in the UK charts. It happened with such lightning speed that it seemed like the Hit Factory had gone into overdrive. Within the space of two months we had written a song, made the record, promoted and marketed it and waved it off to the top of the charts.

The quickest anyone could write, record, produce and promote a record these days is no less than six months. That's the time it now takes to get a finished CD in your hand with the star's picture on the sleeve. Most of the time is taken up with getting television and radio exposure lined up as nobody wants to move without pre-marketing the product. A record company needs to know what their returns will be, and they are too frightened to put out a CD without knowing for sure that the fans will like it. They can't afford to have the public say 'No' – not when they've just paid £80 million for the artist. You have to force a record on people through marketing. Never mind the quality – feel the width!

●

The demand for material for both Jason and Kylie was almost overwhelming, and at the same time as writing for them I was also writing for Sonia, Donna Summer, Big Fun and others, so it was a constant stream of writing and recording. I'd be writing songs in every spare moment. These days when most people sit down they put on the television or radio; nobody really sits and thinks. I find a lot of peace and creativity by sitting in silence and thinking. It occurs to me that we never stop to listen to our bodies. We get swamped with sensory input.

I found myself commuting around the world trying to keep up. I flew to Melbourne to meet Jason armed with more songs, intending to work on his first album *Ten Good Reasons* and do some more follow-up work with Kylie.

MEL & KIM
SHOWING OUT

SUPET 107

ABOVE: Mel & Kim were a fantastic double act. They knew how to have fun and could sing and dance with tremendous energy. The loss of Mel to cancer at the tender age of 21 was deeply felt by everyone at the Hit Factory.

LEFT: Donna Summer was one of the most professional singers I ever had the good fortune to work with. She hit each note perfectly, and hearing her perform my songs was a flattering and rewarding experience.

Princess
"I'LL KEEP ON LOVING YOU"

ABOVE: Princess (aka Desirée Heslop) started out as a backing singer, but her vocal talents were soon spotted in our studio, and soon we had put out her debut single, Say I'm Your Number One.

ABOVE: Rick Astley became synonymous with Stock Aitken Waterman. He was the boy next door who became a superstar. Yet Matt Aitken and I took some convincing that he really had what it takes. He did!

RIGHT: *Although critics proclaimed that SAW records had a distinctive sound, our stable of artists was surprisingly diverse. This typical 'Best Of' album showcased the talents of crooner Rick Astley, pop divas Bananarama and Sinitta and house stylists Mel & Kim.*

RIGHT: *As SAW's reputation grew, more and more artists wanted to work with us, including soap stars Kylie Minogue and Jason Donovan and original boy band Brother Beyond.*

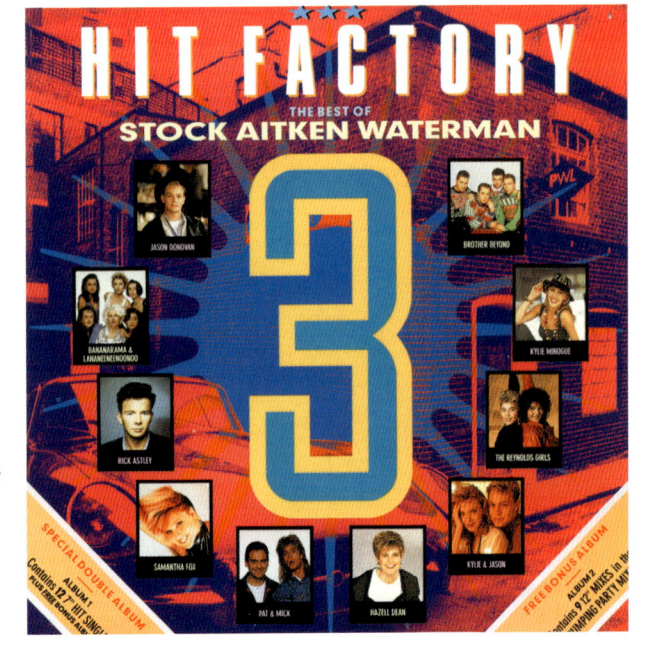

Both he and Kylie were very busy in *Neighbours* and it was difficult to get session time with them. I had unexpected spare time and soon discovered the Australian youth's beach-orientated lifestyle. I got the distinct impression most young Australians wished they were really Californians, and they had a kind of resentment towards Old Mother England.

But it wasn't part of my schedule to spend hours having barbies on the beach. There was work to be done. On arrival in Melbourne I managed to record a single with Kylie, but I also spent a pleasant social evening with her and her family. Jason came too and we chilled out and watched videos. Jason and Kylie were 'an item' in real life, too, although I was a bit slow to notice. When it was time for me to go back to the hotel, Jason and Kylie left together. It still didn't occur to me they were in love. They kept it all secret and it was part of their game with the press. I was so busy producing hit records about love that Kylie and Jason's true-life romance passed me by.

> **KYLIE AND JASON'S TRUE-LIFE ROMANCE PASSED ME BY**

In April 1989 Jason Donovan quit his role in *Neighbours* so he could concentrate on pop music. At the Hit Factory I did two albums with Jason. The first one was released in the summer of 1989 and went five times platinum. I wrote most of the songs, although we did one cover, which was Brian Hyland's *Sealed With A Kiss*. Jason's singing career really took off and he had many hits during 1989, including *When You Come Back To Me* and *Every Day (I Love You More)*. Kylie's other hits that year were *Hand On Your Heart* and *Wouldn't Change A Thing*. In 1990 she was back in the charts with *Tears On My Pillow* and *Better The Devil You Know*, while Jason did *Hang on to Your Love* and went on a hugely successful world tour.

Jason became one of the most popular artists in British pop history, with fans screaming and blocking the streets every time he made a public appearance. He was voted 'Best Male Singer' and 'Most Fanciable Male' in polls for magazines such as *Smash Hits*.

Although the SAW team worked hard round the clock, our artists were mainly young kids out to enjoy themselves. A bit of pot smoking went in the corner of the Australian studio, but that was something I never approved of. If it had been my studio I would have kicked them out. Kylie was never involved, but Jason and his mates would occasionally light up a spliff. We never allowed pot in our studio in London. I don't moralize about drugs, it's just something I have never been into.

The night after I'd finished recording Kylie's first album back in the UK, I went out with Kylie and her mother to have a couple of beers, which was more my kind of thing. It was Easter Sunday, 1988. There'd been nobody else in the studio but Kylie and me, and her mum dutifully waited for her in reception. It was about 9pm when we finished the album and we thought we'd go off and celebrate. Kylie wanted to go to Stringfellows in the West End. I was wearing a pair of ripped jeans and they wouldn't let me in. I created a big fuss at the door and told them I was with Kylie Minogue and did the classic, 'Don't you know who I am?'. Of course it didn't make a blind bit of difference. Eventually they let us in through the back door. So we sat at the bar and had a drink. Normally, at the local pub, I might drink a couple of draught lagers, but at Stringfellows they served strong bottled beer.

After Kylie went back to her hotel with her mum, I drove home down the A2 to Kent in my flashy new Jaguar. I was in a hurry to see my wife Bobbie, who was pregnant with our second child. As I went to overtake a car, its driver decided to speed up. We were driving in tandem and he wouldn't let me pass. So I put my foot down and shot ahead. At that moment the police pulled out of a side road and saw me speeding. They pulled me over and said they could smell alcohol on my breath. They took a roadside breathalyzer test, which proved positive. At the police station they carried out more tests, which showed I was a borderline case. I could either give a blood or urine sample for verification, but they weren't set up for testing urine so I'd have to wait three hours for a doctor to arrive for a blood test. I didn't want to spend all night in a police cell. So I just signed a form and accepted I was over the limit. There wasn't much choice as I wanted to get home.

I later appeared at Bexley magistrates court, where they said I'd been driving at 120mph. However, I managed to avoid prosecution. When I came out a local reporter recognized me and asked if she could write the headline: 'He should be so lucky.' I asked her not to print it, as I wasn't proud of the incident. And, for some reason, she didn't.

●

Although we all had the occasional drink, Jason and Kylie weren't party animals in the old-fashioned rock'n'roll sense. I was glad about that. It was such a cliché. I always thought that anybody who chucked a television through a hotel window or wore make-up on stage and played long guitar solos was really boring. That was a hackneyed pastiche of old 1970s ideas. I reckon Stock Aitken Waterman were the ones bucking the trend. Everyone else was following a well-worn route. We were the outrageous rebels because we didn't do anything the critics liked. If the music press hated us so much, surely in a way it was more 'rock'n'roll' to stand up and defy them?

While they enjoyed leisure time when they could, it should be stressed that Jason and Kylie were both highly professional artists who took their work very seriously. Kylie, in particular, had a lot of steel under that soft exterior and she knew exactly where she was going and what she was doing. Even during her leisure time, Kylie engaged in a pursuit that seemed to require concentration and dedication. Kylie liked to crochet

KYLIE LIKED TO CROCHET

– while Jason surfed. She really did. She sat in the studio and did crochet work in between takes. She was making booties and scarves, for friends' babies I guess. It was quite therapeutic. It's like doing a crossword puzzle to keep your mind focused.

When I went back to Australia for a second time to work on Jason's album, he was already very much into the idea of playing music as an alternative to an acting career. Jason loved to hang out with us in the studio. My aim was always to get a song done quickly and get home, but Jason used to want to hang out and jam. He could play the guitar okay, but we were making pop songs, not guitar rock. When we finished work and the album was released it shot to Number One and stayed there for three weeks.

In a sense we were the stars on those records, because Matt and I wrote the songs and played all the instruments, with the exception of the odd saxophone. Pete wouldn't come into the studio very often, usually just to listen to the latest mix. I needed Matt for his musical skills, although it is very difficult to write songs with somebody else. As Paul Gambaccini once said, 'There are two things in life you can do with one other person that are highly intimate, and the other one is to write a song.' Because I'd known Matt for years we were close enough for songwriting to be possible. Even so, I still found it very difficult.

Meanwhile, thanks to SAW, the world was going Kylie and Jason mad. They made an appealing couple and had tremendous charm. In her vulnerability, Kylie reminded me of Judy Garland. Jason was in love with her and he went through the wringer emotionally after she dropped him and started dating Michael Hutchence of INXS. Jason was also under pressure because of the kind of records he was making with us. They were huge hits, but his peers were always ready to criticize and put him right. In Australia you either liked INXS or Midnight Oil – at least that's how Jason explained it to me. And, of course, he was doing this 'pop stuff' and his mates were teasing him.

Amazingly, the 'mates down the pub' influenced almost every single pop star we ever worked with. Thanks to the mates down the pub, the artist would start saying, 'I want to do something heavier – not this pop stuff.' Their influence was incredulous to us because *none* of their so-called mates was ever successful. They just had ordinary jobs, but they always had their bloody opinions about music. The pop star was having hits all over the world, yet 'the mates' were forever mouthing off about what we were doing wrong. This kind of attitude swayed poor old Jason. It was peer pressure and you can't underestimate its effects, particularly when the victim is young.

Kylie and Jason became targets. You need a really thick skin when you are only in your early twenties and people are telling you you're rubbish. Today, however, Kylie is thought of as a cultural icon and a pop goddess – but Jason didn't survive so well in the pop world. This was partly the result of an unfortunate episode in 1992 when the British magazine *The Face* tried to 'out' him as a homosexual. In my opinion, the magazine's campaign was motivated by envy. If they could destroy his sexual appeal, Jason's audience of young girls would desert him.

It all started when a militant gay group launched a campaign that involved flyposting images of celebrities they alleged were gay. *The Face* wrote an article about the campaign and reproduced one of the posters. Jason wasn't homophobic but he didn't like the implication that he was concealing something. Jason decided to sue *The Face* over the article, perhaps after receiving some bad advice. When he asked my advice, I told him not to sue and to take it as a compliment – some of the finest artists, singers and creative people in the world are gay. But he was somehow persuaded not to let the magazine get away with calling him gay.

He sued the magazine, won the case and was awarded £200,000 in damages. He returned most of the money to save the magazine, which was now threatened with closure. Despite this, the media called him homophobic. It destroyed his career and he lost his fans, many of whom were gay and took his legal action as an affront.

Jason should have shrugged his shoulders and laughed. Our records were a big hit in the gay community and as a result some people assumed that

Matt and I were gay. I've never been offended by it because I'm quite secure in my own sexuality. My assessment of gay men is that they tend to be sensitive and like songs that move them. That's different from young bucks, male heteros who like thrashing guitars and being aggressive. I don't knock that approach, but my songs have always been about human relationships, love and romance, loss and longing. And they are emotional subjects that have always appealed to gay men and to women.

If 20 per cent of the male population is gay and 50 per cent of the entire population is female – then, as songwriters, we've got at least 60 per cent on our side! I've always kept away from the strutting male rock music that groups such as Guns N' Roses and Iron Maiden play. If it's all down to style and no content then I'm not interested. There are two types of hits. One is a record and one is a song. You can have a hit record built round lots of guitar riffs, which may have lots of excitement but you couldn't say it was a great song.

I managed to connect with gay record buyers only because their tastes happened to coincide with mine. We spotted that record companies were rather condescending towards the gay market. They were chucking out cheap and cheerful stuff in the hope that it would appeal to gay men. We wanted to do something that was better quality. If we put out a decent song, we thought 60 per cent of the market would respond, and they did.

●

Jason is now a parent with two children and he has found his feet with a successful acting career in the theatre, film and television. His theatre career began just before *The Face* libel case, when he was offered an opportunity to play Joseph in the stage show *Joseph and the Amazing Technicolor Dreamcoat*, devised by Tim Rice and Andrew Lloyd Webber. At that point Jason was signed to our label and we agreed to write a more up-to-date song that could be added to the show specifically for Jason. We had a meeting with Sir Andrew at his house in Eaton Square, and agreed to write songs to go into the show if we had the rights to release the singles. Lloyd Webber agreed in principle, but when we came to do the deal he informed us that Tim Rice objected. He thought the show was perfect and didn't need updating.

We went to the opening night in June 1991 and Jason did very well and got rave reviews. The show at the London Palladium was completely sold out. He also had a hit single in 1991 with *Any Dream Will Do* from the musical, which was his fourth Number One. *Happy Together* was his last single for PWL, after which he signed to Polydor. But the court case affected his career and record sales fell to the point where his new label eventually dropped him. *Joseph* closed in 1994 and Jason spent the next few years living it up and quickly losing his 'boy next door' image.

He went on to appear in *The Rocky Horror Show* in the UK, brilliantly, and ironically, playing the role of camp Dr Frank N. Furter. Back in Australia he landed a role in the hit television drama *MDA*, where he has gone from strength to strength. He recently returned to the London stage to star in *Chitty Chitty Bang Bang* at the London Palladium. But I believe going into the theatre damaged him as a pop star, and he came to be seen as a 'luvvie'.

Jason must have realized that suing *The Face* was a bad move. I wish he hadn't done it. He always said that the court action was not about his sexuality but about the right to a private life. Yet people always want to pull you down when you're a star, and he was in line for a few personal attacks. He suffered vilification as well as peer pressure, and Jason Donovan's pop career with SAW was over.

HITS AND MISSES

It wasn't all Rick, Kylie and Jason coming through the doors of the Hit Factory though. A few artists Pete found turned out to be impossible to handle. There was no way we could work with them, which caused a few hair-raising moments. It becomes very intense in a recording studio, especially if the artist lacks talent, or is just plain crazy.

Generally we had a good working relationship with our artists, and problems usually only arose when somebody didn't like a haircut or the skirt or make-up they were wearing on the video. None of us got involved with photos or video shoots – we were too busy writing songs, making records and selling hits. Videos were David Howells' department. The videos cost £200,000–300,000 to make – while the records cost a fraction of that.

We had a good working relationship with Sinitta, with whom we had a number of hits. She was born Sinitta Renet Malone in 1966 in Washington DC, the daughter of disco singer Miquel Brown. She appeared in stage musicals from an early age and released her first singles in 1983, so we knew what she could do vocal-wise – she also had fantastic legs. As soon as I saw them, I knew she was a great singer!

A&R man Simon Cowell signed her to his Fanfare label, and with our help from 1986 onwards she had four Top Ten hits, including *So Macho/Cruising* (1986), *Toy Boy* (1987), *Cross My Broken Heart* (1988) and *Right Back Where We Started From* (1989). We didn't write *So Macho* or *Right Back Where We Started From* but we did write the others, including her other famous hit *Toy Boy*. Some reviewers thought she had a sexy voice, and what Sinitta really wanted to do was to sing soul.

It has been said that SAW dropped Sinitta in favour of Kylie Minogue. However, Sinitta was never on the PWL label, she was always on Simon's Fanfare label, and by the time Kylie came along in 1988 we were all moving on. Sinitta had made it clear that she wanted to do a different kind of music. She had a good voice and she certainly could sing soul, but that wasn't what the public wanted at the time. I feel that a covenant exists between an artist and the public, which an artist should not break, or they won't get the public's support again.

Sinitta wanted to reinvent herself. Madonna manages to do that by doing exactly the same thing all the time while wearing a different frock or using different make-up and slicking back her hair. Many artists try at some point to change their image. Comedians try to go 'straight' and become serious actors. Typecast actors cut off trademark hairstyles or have a face job. But reinvention rarely works – especially in the case of chart pop stars.

●

There were plenty of occasions during the heyday of SAW when I feared we'd never get anywhere in our daily struggle to get hits out. We often had to deal with the most extraordinary characters in our quest to deliver the goods. A good example was Carol Hitchcock, a singer who flitted past our window one day and flitted off again. In 1987 we did a synth-thumping cover of Motown song *Get Ready* with her. It was written by Smokey Robinson and had been a hit for The Temptations.

Carol was a striking woman: Australian, bald and a bit of a body-builder. I felt she was a bit frightening, to be honest! Maybe that's why her record only just scraped into the Top 60 in Australia and the UK. The B-side of Carol's record was *More Than Words Can Say*, a SAW composition that was later resurrected for a Mel & Kim album track, but alas we couldn't resurrect Ms Hitchcock's record career.

> **I FELT SHE WAS A BIT FRIGHTENING**

Sadly, we weren't any more successful with Suzette Charles. She was very attractive and had won a Miss America contest. Suzette had a black mother and an Italian father, which gave her considerable exotic appeal and sophistication. She was signed to RCA America and said she wanted to work with SAW. I did six or seven songs with her, the bulk of an album, and they were to be put out on RCA in Britain. But as the label had no investment in the project they were not prepared to help make it a success for RCA America. It was a very competitive arrangement, so it didn't work out. I thought she was great and could have been highly successful. We recorded another song called *After You've Gone* but we never finished the record.

SAW worked with many glamorous female singers, but one area that SAW pioneered was the development of acts who came from outside the normal run of the music industry. The days of simply signing up four-piece guitar bands from the local pub were over and we were interested in people who already had an established appeal with their target audience.

One such act was the highly popular duo Pat & Mick. We did a whole string of records with them over a number of years. Pat Sharp and Mick Brown were Capital Radio DJs and television presenters by day and made pop songs by night. It all came about when we were asked to make some charity records in aid of the charity Help A London Child. We produced loads of records with Pat & Mick, which were all big hits, and we ended up giving the charity a cheque for £300,000.

At the same time we began working with girl groups such as The Dolly Dots, who had started out in Holland in 1979 as a group of dancers, and went on to have big hits with *Boys*, *Radio* and *Rollerskating*. The Dolly Dots were huge in Holland but were keen to break the rest of Europe, so they came to SAW for help. We did a song for them in 1987 called *What A Night*, which was a hit in Holland, but didn't really make it anywhere else. The girls were so disappointed they broke up the following year, although they got back together for a one-off reunion some years later.

We had more luck with The Reynolds Girls, although we only had one record, one release and one hit. The girls were 18-year-old Linda Reynolds and her 16-year-old sister Aisling. They were from Liverpool and were of Irish ancestry. Linda was a hairdresser who gave up her job to be a singer; Aisling dropped out of school to join her. They pestered Pete to hear their demo when he was recording his weekly radio show in Liverpool and he gave in. He liked the demo and decided to send the girls down to us at the Hit Factory.

We came up with a song for them called *I'd Rather Jack*. I believe the idea came from a remark made by Matt in the studio. Everyone was talking about Fleetwood Mac, and he said, 'I'd rather jack than Fleetwood Mac.' I think 'the jack' was a dance craze going round at the time. Pete also said we should have a go at those radio DJs who wouldn't play our records. So the lyric goes: 'Golden oldies, Rolling Stones, we don't want them back. I'd rather jack than Fleetwood Mac.' That was the chorus. The verse was a dig at the prevailing regime of DJs who were old enough to be the girls' fathers and yet were in charge of all the music we heard on the radio. Yet they must have played it because it was a big Top Ten hit in 1989.

I'd Rather Jack spent 12 weeks on the UK charts and got to Number Eight. The girls became favourites with the public but they got a bit too big for their boots and parted company with SAW – not a wise move. They decided to release their next record, *Get Real,* on their own label and it failed to chart, so it was goodnight to The Reynolds Girls.

We also worked with disco divas The Three Degrees when they were signed to the Supreme label. The R&B vocal trio from Philadelphia featured Fayette Pinkney, Sheila Ferguson and Valerie Holiday. They were, of course, much more important than The Dolly Dots or The Reynolds

THEY GOT A BIT TOO BIG FOR THEIR BOOTS

Hits and Misses 75

Girls. They'd had some major hits back in the 1970s, including *Maybe* and *When Will I See You Again*; they are even said to be Prince Charles's favourite disco group. However, they were on a downward slope in their career when we met them and Sheila Ferguson was desperately trying to pull their career back together. I wrote a song for them called *Heaven I Need*, which we struggled to put out.

Lonnie Gordon was another American singer who came to us thanks to our contacts with Nick East. She was a soul diva and had a strong reputation in the clubs. She was in need of a hit record, which we were happy to supply. I wrote a song called *Happening All Over Again*, which was a Top Five single in 1990. I always looked out for the latest trends in music and at the time we worked with Lonnie there was a trend called Italiano house, with big pianos playing sultry Latin rhythms in the background. Her song was produced in that style and was quite a success.

I worked with a lot of black artists over the years and I am pleased to say we had hits with all of them. Some people say we only wrote 'blue-eyed pop music', but that was only because our biggest acts were white. One of my all-time favourite artists is Stevie Wonder and it would have been great to have the opportunity of working with him.

Sometimes there was a breakdown of communications in the studio. For example, we worked with Edwin Starr, who was originally from Nashville, Tennessee and moved to England in the 1980s. He had had a big US Number One with the stridently political *War* in 1970, but I first met him when we were doing the Zebrugge charity version of *Let It Be* – Starr was one of the guest vocalists.

Edwin was fantastic in the studio and knew the song backwards. We all got on very well and he was so excited when *Let It Be* went to Number One that he asked if I could produce a song just for him. We were all taken up with the emotion and excitement of the time so I said, 'Yes, fine, have a word with David Howells and work out a deal.'

He came to the studio the next week, and in the meantime I'd written a song for him. I had all the lyrics typed up and printed out and the backing track ready. He seemed impressed and I explained that this was how I always worked. So I put the backing track on and started singing the words to him, but I'd hardly got past the first few notes when he stopped me and said he didn't want to hear the tune because basically his vocal style was to sing ad-lib.

He took the microphone and off we went. He tried to scat the words and, of course, it didn't work because it was a structured song. It had chord changes and movements, and wasn't just a series of 'get on down, get on ups'. Edwin soon realized this and knew he had to learn the tune for it to work. He got through it eventually, but it wasn't very good. It turned out that I was better at writing songs and he was better at vamping.

They say girls have more fun, but boy bands were becoming the big new trend of the late 1980s and they really boomed in the 1990s after the success of Take That. We worked with several such bands, including Big Fun – three blond kids desperate for stardom. We had a couple of hits with them, including *Blame It On The Boogie,* which was originally a Jackson Five song, and our own *Can't Shake The Feeling.* But soon it was all over and they'd had their moment in the spotlight.

It's sad but true that some of our artists got left behind. Sometimes the artists can be their own worst enemies. They don't see the big picture, or else people confuse them with conflicting advice. They end up not knowing who to trust or where to turn. They might see Matt and I writing them a hit song but not really

THEY THINK THAT IF MIKE AND MATT CAN DO IT, SO CAN THEY

understand how it happened or what forces were unleashed to get them into the charts. They think that if Mike and Matt can do it, so can they, on their own and without help, and when it doesn't work out, they are devastated. Expectations are raised too high by one hit record. The artist dreams of lasting fame and fortune. It's possible to achieve both, but never guaranteed.

And when the shouting is over and a new wave are waiting to take their place in the charts and on *Top Of The Pops,* an often grim future beckons. The former pop idols are left to fend for themselves. It's wrong. Business is business but the artists are only human and should be treated better.

Many young singers thought they were stars in the making when the real talent was coming from Matt and me. As with all strong personalities, there were bound to be clashes, but some of the stars were meek as lambs compared to Matt and me – we were the ones who really threw tantrums! On a bad day I would scream and shout and we would have a real go at each other. But a studio is a fraught place. You work under a lot of pressure. To get people going you have to shout sometimes. Faced with a tough job, Matt would sometimes light a fag, put his feet up and go to sleep. I don't deal with stress in the same way.

> **WE WERE THE ONES WHO REALLY THREW TANTRUMS!**

I never gave up on a song. It might be a case of trying to get the lyrics to hang together and pull in the right direction. When it came to recording, we might do a mix that nobody liked. I would mix a recording 150 times or more to get it right and then say, 'Okay, let's change that bass line.' There was no point in hanging on to a bass line that wasn't working, even if we had invested two hours in recording it. If something wasn't working, I'd be ruthless. It might mean doing a song 50 different ways. It might mean spending weeks and weeks on one aspect of one song to get it to work. That put a big strain on the mixing engineers. But it was these behind-the-scenes battles that ensured SAW products were always full of energy.

SVENGALIS OF POP

After our enormous success with artists such as Jason Donovan, Kylie Minogue and Rick Astley, critics started calling SAW puppeteers, the 'Svengalis* of pop'. I hated that – it made us sound menacing and mysterious. Yet there was a degree of truth in it, in as much as we, as songwriters, helped create the stars and their images.

When a new client headed our way, Pete, Matt and I would always talk around the 'problem': we had to work out how to sell the artist. It usually started with a discussion about our schedule. Pete would say to me and Matt:

'We've got Mel & Kim coming in next.'

'Okay, so what are we gonna do for them?'

'I want you to write a classic.'

'Oh right. How much of a classic? A full classic or just a partial one?'

'Just write a Number One.'

It was a fatuous comment, but that was when the real work would begin. Matt and I would discuss the sort of song we could write that would be most suitable for Mel & Kim. There couldn't be any love interest, not with two girls in the act. So we avoided the issue and wrote a lyric about East End girls putting on their make-up, going out and having a good time. That wasn't a manufactured image, that was something the girls used to do. When we came up with their hit *Showing Out* we were responding to real lives and personalities.

The girls were easy. Rick Astley really had been a problem – not as an individual, because he truly was 'the boy next door'. Rick was fresh-faced

---

* *Svengali was the villain in George du Maurier's 1894 novel* Trilby, *who exercised sinister powers over the heroine, the young singer Trilby.*

and young and we didn't want to do anything too raunchy or rock'n'roll with him; we wanted to tread carefully. In the end, his image was down to his management and record company; Pete also had considerable involvement. Matt and I helped in other ways. A big part of our philosophy was to make records for smart working people who like to dress up to go out, and our Rick Astley songs always bore that in mind.

It's cool for the Metropolitan chic to wear torn jeans and go to exclusive London clubs looking tatty. But people who have finished a hard day's work in a shop, factory or warehouse want to put on their best clothes for their night out. They were the people we were aiming at. That's why Pete insisted Rick Astley wore a suit. He didn't want him to wear a funny hat and look weird. Pete came under pressure to make him trendier, but he stuck to his guns. He wanted Rick to look ordinary, but smart. Matt and I didn't get involved in this peripheral yet important process. David Howells organized photo sessions and approved the image of an artist, but ultimately the principal image was laid down by Stock Aitken Waterman in the studio through our songs and production.

Yet even the most powerful and mystical of skills couldn't make Rick Astley into the new Elvis. That's why I objected to being called a Svengali, though I could see how Pete might have deserved the name. It was around this time that Pete started sounding off about knowing more about pop music than anybody else. He made a big thing about how good Stock Aitken Waterman were, while I thought we should have been a bit more self-effacing. And when Pete launched the PWL label it looked as though the dreaded Svengalis were taking over the world.

PWL certainly had a controversial lift-off. We signed Bill Wyman's future wife Mandy Smith in 1987 and she was the first artist to have a record out on the PWL label with *I Just Can't Wait*. David Howells brought her into the company after she had received lots of publicity for her relationship with Bill Wyman. David said, 'You can't buy this kind of publicity.' I wasn't happy with the idea. Mandy was a beautiful, lovely girl, but she was very young – just 17 – and I didn't think she was particularly talented in the singing department. As it turned out, the record wasn't successful – it only reached 91 in the charts – and it was a rare example of SAW not coming up with a hit. It seemed the public wouldn't accept the idea of such a young girl being involved with a famous rock veteran.

Nevertheless, Mandy and Bill did marry in 1989, and we, along with a host of celebrities and photographers, attended their grand wedding. There was a flight of steps into the reception so you could see who was arriving. Bill's old friend Spike Milligan turned up quite late and made a spectacular entrance carrying his wedding present for 53-year old Bill: a Zimmer frame.

The mid-1980s was a period of rapid expansion as our 'assembly line' worked overtime. We developed a second studio downstairs at The Borough, where another team of producers working for PWL was set to operate. The big difference was that upstairs Stock Aitken Waterman could write as well as produce the records. Another asset was that I could sing tunes to the artists in the studio, so they could get the idea for their next hit. We never made demos. In the record business people are always talking about demonstration discs. Why bother? Why not just make the record? If Bananarama was due in for a session, Matt and I would write a song, then I'd sing it to the girls and we'd all go into the studio and cut it. No problem. No demos.

> **WE NEVER MADE DEMOS. WHY BOTHER? WHY NOT JUST MAKE THE RECORD?**

There was another reason why we didn't really need to make demos. It was the era when producers moved rapidly from using acoustic pianos, acoustic guitars and drums to synthesizers, drum machines and samples. It wasn't always an easy transition, although the new technology gave us the means to create perfect sounds and instant hits. The music was sequenced on computers and in the early days of computers it was difficult to reliably save material. Despite all the hype about technology, it was frustrating when you had to spend a whole day trying to get one tone on a tape that was needed to control the timing of all the instruments.

We were still using two-inch 24-track tape. Around 1988 we began using Sony 48-track half-inch tape. We were somewhere between hardware and software. We weren't fully into computer software until the mid-1990s. It was essential to keep up to date, though, because if you let technology beat you you might as well stay in bed. Today, the technical revolution in the studio is virtually complete and the man with the mouse is king.

Cutting-edge technology was vital to the success of our operation, but we still needed great tunes and catchy lyrics. I wouldn't want to destroy people's belief that it all happens by magic, or that you sit there with a quill pen writing dots on a score. You used the technology, but the song came first.

When The Beatles started recording, technology was developing very quickly and electronic instruments were already in the pipeline. There was a whole world of possibilities waiting to be explored, possibilities that were fully checked out during the 1960s and '70s. By the time SAW started out, most of the big ideas had already been done: Paul McCartney had worked with a string quartet on *Yesterday* – no one had tried that in pop music before – and The Beach Boys with Brian Wilson and progressive rock groups had all tried to create new sounds, often using electronic keyboards.

This didn't stop our own quest for perfection and new sounds, however. It would become a daily obsession to come up with fresh ideas and bring them to fruition at the Hit Factory. When I came up with *This Time I Know It's For Real* for Donna Summer it was a real 'eureka' moment. Like Archimedes, the idea came to me while I was sitting in the bath. By the time my hair was dry I had the basic tune, and during the drive to the studio I got the first verse and chorus. Then Matt and I worked together to get the song down on tape. The final piece of the jigsaw was when the star came in to lay down the vocals. After Donna Summer had left, we finished the track. That song splashed down at Number Seven on the US Billboard chart in 1989. Once again, it confirmed my faith in SAW. I felt like part of a fighting music machine that was ready for battle. Give us the tools and we'd finish the job!

We achieved some spectacular results on the pop battlefield. Our increasing market share was the result of hard work rather than hype. We knew exactly what we were doing and who we were aiming at. You can't convince the public to buy 800,000 copies of a single unless they really want to. Yet there was so much hostility towards us it became embarrassing. Even other artists joined the snipers from the press and the grumblers from the record industry. Heavy metal singer Bruce Dickinson ranted about us on stage at Iron Maiden concerts. We were flattered at first, but the reaction got worse as we got fitter, stronger and more and more successful.

Andrew Loog Oldham once described the record business as the 'industry of human happiness'. Oldham was the man who discovered the Rolling Stones and set up Immediate, one of Britain's first independent pop labels in 1965. The label's 'happiness' slogan might have seemed rather overblown, but it had a resonance and started a credo. I've always seen my role as a musician as being that of making other people happy, too. It may seem obvious, but music really is a universal provider of fun. Pop music fulfils this function brilliantly and embraces both art and commerce in a way that has affected millions of lives and has created a billion-dollar worldwide industry.

It still seems extraordinary to me that simply humming a tune that has sprung like a phantom into the mind sparks off a process that brings so much pleasure and profit to so many. You can't visualize a song as it hangs in the air, but you can certainly see the physical results. And they are HUGE. A vast army of people is employed in an enterprise that now spans the globe. When most people talk about 'industry' they imagine tangible assets like mines, factories and steel works, but the ephemeral world of pop has its own kind of substance.

First among the key elements is the recording studio, with its expert staff of writers, producers, singers, musicians and sound engineers. They are the front-line workers engaged in the sweat and toil of extracting the raw material – the hit records. Behind them are the ancillary staff, the clerks, secretaries and receptionists. Then there are those twin pillars of the music establishment, the record companies and music publishers, each with their own management structures, A&R departments and back-up personnel.

Behind them are accountants, lawyers, managers, promoters, booking agents and publicists. Add to them experts in fields ranging from marketing and corporate strategy to copyright and exploitation of back catalogue. Then there is the specialist music media, which employs journalists, photographers and the world of broadcasting, film and video, each with its DJs, producers and directors. All that's without even including the army of groups, composers and artists of an infinite variety of style and genre.

There are performers and bands that have been performing since what seems like the dawn of time. Added to the heaving mass of veteran artists, from the Rolling Stones to Bob Dylan and Rod Stewart, we have an endless succession of new hopefuls all determined to make their mark. There are those freshly minted Pop Idols, such as Will Young and Michelle McManus, adroitly brought into play to sustain the British pop market in recent years, and there is now the re-emergence of glam rock, epitomized by groups such as The Darkness.

It might seem like a vast, disparate, sprawling mass of conflicting aims and aspirations. Yet there is one key element that keeps this fuzzy entity focused and together – a great pop song. The bottom line – when all the arguing and debate is over – is that everyone needs a hit. All those people engaged in so many diverse activities desperately need the adrenalin rush of a smash hit record to keep the business on track and functioning. In other words – they'd all be out of a job without me and my fellow hit writers!

When I write a song I like to think about what the public will buy as well as what a record company will like. The industry needs to like the record because they control television and radio, and without their backing it won't get any airplay. But when SAW was at its peak, the taste of the general public was always our guiding principle. The industry didn't have the same stranglehold then that it does now. When I set up my own label it remained my ambition to give people the kind of music they really wanted to hear. Of course, I wanted to make money too, but what I most enjoy about the pop business is discovering new young talent and giving it a platform. That's the big buzz and it's what the music industry should be about, as opposed to ruthlessly exploiting talent.

Sadly, the process of creating 'stars' is not always a happy one. Indeed, we could just as easily call it the 'industry of human unhappiness'. I could produce a list of hundreds of people who were thrust into the limelight, did their record company's bidding and then got dumped. People say, 'You've had your fifteen minutes of fame, so what are you complaining about?' That's a very irresponsible attitude. SAW never managed any acts, so we really weren't Svengalis.

Although the artists couldn't always see it, by aiming to make records quickly and, therefore, cheaply, we were looking after their best interests. We didn't spend months using up studio time, for which the artists would have had to pay. Our aim was to write a song and get the artist in and out in the shortest possible time. Some artists resented that. They wanted to spend time hanging out in the studio doing what they believed rock stars did. But our methods not only saved them money but also gave them hits from which they

> **WHEN I WRITE A SONG I THINK ABOUT WHAT THE PUBLIC WILL BUY AS WELL AS WHAT A RECORD COMPANY WILL LIKE**

made money. Our message was clear: 'Go away and enjoy yourself. We'll take care of the production.'

Nobody made cheaper records than SAW. The cost of producing Number One platinum singles was minimal. Established artists might spend six months making a record that sells the same as some of ours sold, but they will spend half their profits on recording costs.

I also advised artists not to stay in expensive hotels, not to travel everywhere by taxi or limousine, and to shoot their video in Wapping rather than Los Angeles. It was their money that was spent on these luxuries, but many of them didn't realize that.

It's nice to think that Kylie Minogue in particular may have benefited from our sound advice. She is now said to have a £30million fortune, which includes a string of properties in Melbourne and homes in London and Paris. Kylie is now one of the world's richest women. And it all started with *I Should Be So Lucky*. After all, she was only earning £150 an episode when she was Charlene in *Neighbours*. After Kylie hooked up with Stock Aitken Waterman she gained a fortune of £5.25 million from singles' sales alone.

If 1988 was a good year for us, 1989 was ten times better. We had seven Number One hits that year with six different artists, and 15 Top Fives. It was an astonishing fact that we were having more hits than The Beatles in their heyday, and more Number Ones. However, they had written mainly for themselves and only put out one album and three singles a year. SAW were putting out 30 to 40 singles a year. Nobody would say we were bigger and better than The Beatles, but we certainly had more hits. Kylie Minogue's singles alone sold up to 700,000 copies every time. To put this in context, a Number One record in 2003 would sell no more than 30,000 copies, while the average chart record now sells about 10,000 copies. We got through a huge amount of work in 1989. During that year, I wrote seven albums' worth of songs and made the same number of records.

Svengalis of Pop

There is no doubt Stock Aitken Waterman was a phenomenon that only now is being given its true recognition. Night after night on music television channels you see programmes extolling the virtues of the 1980s and SAW's contribution to pop. We had many awards given to us by the music industry at the time, albeit I suspect somewhat grudgingly. After all they couldn't ignore us, even if certain elements within the industry were alarmed at our chart dominance.

One of our proudest moments was winning the Ivor Novello Awards, which are presented annually by the British Academy Of Composers and Songwriters. The 'Ivors' are among the most prestigious awards in the industry and are named after the great British songwriter Ivor Novello (1893–1951), who was also an actor and dramatist. Novello was born in Cardiff and educated at Oxford University, where he became a chorister. He wrote *Keep The Home Fires Burning*, which was a big hit during the First World War.

Lennon and McCartney won the 'Songwriter Of The Year' award twice, but we are the only composers to have won it three times in a row, from 1988 to 1990. In the third year, to prevent it becoming too political, they gave us a joint award with George Michael. In April 1988 SAW won three Ivor Novello Awards including 'Songwriter Of The Year,' 'Most Performed Work' for *This Time I Know It's For Real* and 'Best Selling A-Side' for *Too Many Broken Hearts*.

At the BPI Brit Awards of 1987 we won 'Best Producers', and although we were far more successful as producers in 1988 and 1989, for some reason we never got a mention in those years – perhaps they didn't want to keep giving us awards over and over again. All in all, we won eight Ivors between us, as well as dozens of *Music Week* awards presented by the trade paper.

Behind these impressive staistics and awards, however, there were other factors that seriously began to affect my personal life. During the late

1980s and early 1990s my wife Bobbie raised our three kids almost single-handed. My son Matthew was born in 1982, my son James in 1988 and my daughter Amy in 1992, right throughout the SAW explosion. I was hardly ever at home during the day. I spent all my time in the studio, writing and producing. I would get home at midnight, go to sleep, and after the children had gone off to school in the morning I'd leave for the studio again until late at night.

So I missed the kids' vital formative years, all because I was dedicated to a growing company with many responsibilities. Our staff all had families and mortgages, and they relied on us to get results. We *had* to keep it all going. It was an incredibly stressful time, and not just because of the amount of time I spent in the studio.

Although we were riding the crest of a wave and money was pouring in from the steady flow of SAW hit records, I soon learned that money isn't everything. Although my father had died in 1978, Mother was still alive and she saw the success that he had missed. I know that Dad would have been mighty proud. But there was a downside to my new-found fame and riches that affected Mum and the rest of my family badly. A dark shadow began to fall over my life. It was as unexpected as it was frightening. Just as we were celebrating the first wave of hits with SAW, I began to receive blackmail threats and intimidation from criminal elements.

It began in 1986 — the year that Bananarama went to Number One in America with *Venus*. Everything was going splendidly. I flew out to Miami to record their follow-up single. I was leading a jet-set lifestyle far removed from the days of driving around London in a van with a band. I went to Germany to record with Divine and later went to Paris with Matt to work with heavy metal boys Judas Priest. We didn't release anything with Judas Priest in the end, but they fancied having a go with us as they needed to turn their career round and have a hit single. I think what we did was very good,

Svengalis of Pop 89

but they couldn't live with it. Rob Halford their lead singer had a high-pitched screaming voice and it was all very Spinal Tap. I think they thought we were uncool; I don't think they realized how out of touch they were!

Whatever the weird or unsettling situations you encounter in the music business, at least most of the time it's a good laugh. Yet it was no laughing matter when a face from the past came back to haunt me.

A man I had known during my pub gig days came to see me. The guy had wanted to manage me when I had the band and we had had a loose arrangement, but it didn't really work out because he never found me any work. We had long since gone our separate ways, and in the intervening years he'd ended up down on his luck. He was a bit of a rough diamond and wasn't the sort of guy you'd want to upset. He told me he was sleeping on bare floorboards and that he and his family wouldn't have much of a Christmas that year. It was a rather heavy hint. So I gave him a handout, thinking I was being generous and doing the right thing by an old acquaintance. After all, I'd had a lot of luck, so why not spread some of it around?

A few days later the same man rang me at home and claimed to be in hospital with a collapsed lung. He said some people were demanding money with menaces and had beaten him up. Then he said:

'I've told them that you'll pay.'

'Okay, how much?'

'£300,000.'

'Oh right, really?'

> **A GANG OF THUGS TURNED UP AT MY HOME BRANDISHING WEAPONS**

In no uncertain terms, I told him to go away. The next thing I know Bobbie's calling me in a panic because a gang of thugs had turned up at my family home in Bexley, brandishing weapons and making threats. I was scared, Bobbie was scared. I was forced to employ a round-the-clock bodyguard to look after Bobbie, Matthew and me.

Calming down, I set about trying to find out who or what was behind it. Nothing made sense. I was getting menacing phone calls and strange men were following me everywhere, sitting in cars and watching my movements. The warning was clear enough. They were out to get me. But why? How was I expected to be able to write uplifting jolly pop songs while all this was going on?

I was determined to sort this out one way or another, and as the police proved particularly unhelpful I was forced to arrange a meeting myself with 'the heavies'. I went protected, supported by 14 guys all armed with guns. Their side also turned up for the meeting mob-handed. It was an extremely dangerous situation, but somehow I managed to keep my cool. I just wanted to know why they were coming after me.

It turned out they were employed by East End boxing promoters from whom my 'friend' had previously borrowed money on the grounds that I owed him £300,000. I owed him nothing. He'd apparently given my name as security! Of course, he couldn't pay the money back and they were expecting me to pay off his debt. The worst thing was he'd told them I had refused to pay up. I told them my side of the story.

'All I did was give him £10,000 for his wife to spend at Christmas.'

They looked at me in disbelief: 'You *gave* him £10,000? What for?'

I told them he had been pleading poverty and that I had felt sorry for him and was only trying to help him out. The East End guys went off and sorted him out. I don't know if they ever got their money back; I didn't want to get any more involved. I don't even know what he wanted the money for. It was a period in my life that was very stressful and expensive.

It wasn't over yet. Not long afterwards, in 1988, I received calls from reporters from both the *Sun* and the *Daily Mirror*. They'd been approached by some guy who said he had photographs of my home. He was making blackmail threats, saying that he was going to expose my extravagant lifestyle. I'm a family man, I don't have an extravagant lifestyle, there was no story, but all the same it was frightening.

Next I received threats that someone was going to kidnap my wife and mother and hold them to ransom. This was far worse. My brother-in-law advised me to get my mother out of her home in Folkestone. We had to take her to a safe-house. The kidnap threats were traumatic and upset my mother badly. She was extremely frightened and had to take anti-depressants. We couldn't let her live on her own any more, even though, as it turned out, the threat wasn't serious. She began hallucinating and it sent her into decline.

It was imperative to find out who was behind the threats. It turned out to be an entirely different set of people to those who had plagued me in 1986. It was actually down to an ex-employee. The police eventually dealt with the problem, but the experience toughened me up and made me more streetwise.

Stock Aitken Waterman had become too famous, but as the men behind the music, we didn't have the kind of security around us that most artists take for granted. I was wandering around supermarkets and airports on my own without any protection. I had become like a pop star without realizing it.

I didn't want to be recognized or become a celebrity. None of us was prepared for that kind of attention. Once again it had cost me a lot of money, but you can't take risks where your family's safety is concerned. It forced me to reconsider my entire career. However, after thinking long and hard, I knew that songwriting was what I did best, and my ultimate decision was to carry on working in the industry. I had unquestioning support from Bobbie, which gave me the strength to continue.

Nevertheless, it became increasingly difficult for my family because I was away so often. Shortly after my son James was born in 1988 I was back in Australia working with Kylie and Jason. I had discussed my career path with Bobbie quite early on. I explained that my sole aim was to make a success of my career in the music industry so that I could provide a decent home and financial security. My travels around the world, non-stop working hours in the studio and the downside of fame were the high price we had to pay.

Whatever the pressure I was under, I never ever touched drugs. Like I said, if I was in the control room and an artist lit up a spliff, I'd kick them out. I was absolutely against it, and on grounds more practical than moral. You are taking substances from people who have no scruples. You don't know what you are putting into your system. Why take the risk and what's the point? The music business has been blighted by drug use. You only have to look at the long list of casualties. Personally, I like to be focused and drug-free. I love life; I relish it. I don't want to blot it out. I'd sooner keep fit and do sport and exercise than get stoned.

Yet there is enormous pressure to experiment and consequently risk getting hooked. I never touched the industry's drug of choice, cocaine, even though it can be quite embarrassing to refuse a line of coke in the music business. I remember sitting in a business meeting in 1985 when someone got out a razor and started cutting lines of coke for everyone round the table. I looked at them in bewilderment. A woman cut a line for me, but I told her bluntly, 'I don't want it.' If people are old enough and stupid enough to take drugs, it's their prerogative. I wasn't interested.

Unfortunately cocaine became the currency of the music business during the 1980s; it was a way of getting your record played. 'Just send a gram of coke over to a plugger or DJ and they'll promote your record.' It was pure sleaze. And it was so prevalent in clubs that you began to think you were making records for people who weren't dealing from a full pack.

> **COCAINE BECAME THE CURRENCY OF THE MUSIC BUSINESS DURING THE 1980s**

We were too busy to party. There was no rock'n'roll and drugs for me. I was doing a job that I loved and I wanted to be able to remember as much of it as possible – what's the point of enjoying yourself if you can't remember what you did? I knew I was doing something great and SAW was going to the top. It was a once-in-a-lifetime opportunity. I'd been writing songs since I was a kid and now the public wanted to hear them, so I was making hay. I didn't need drugs to have a great time. But it was a salutary experience to be exposed to the dark side of the music business. I knew then I'd have to be strong and keep my nerve. And there would be even more testing times ahead.

We were swamped with work, but we were earning lots of money. Life was good and should have been simple. It wasn't, and much of this was because of Pete Waterman's self-promotion, which Matt and I kind of encouraged as he was the public face of SAW. Pete had his own television and radio programmes and he was on every chat show and in every magazine. His show for Granada Television, *The Hitman & Her*, was launched in 1989; it featured Pete and Michaela Strachan in a different disco setting each week. Despite getting a pasting from television critics, it proved extremely popular and drew good ratings. That was fine, but Pete's increasingly arrogant attitude was putting the industry's back up.

He was perfectly entitled to speak his mind on any matter that took his fancy. However, Matt and I didn't agree with most of what he said, mainly because it was stirring up so much antagonism. The public gave us their support by buying the records, but we got the opposite from the music industry. As it turned out, there were more serious reasons for this lack of support than Pete's outspoken barbed comments.

By the end of 1989, the three of us in SAW had 27 per cent of the market in the record business. As a result, we were perceived as a major thorn in the side of EMI, BMG and the major companies who had

American, Japanese and German paymasters. They were looking at market shares and asking awkward questions of their crestfallen employees. 'How can three guys in their own studio take 27 per cent of the market, when we are paying you £1million salaries and you employ 7,000 people? What's going on?'

What we didn't need in this delicate situation was Pete going around criticizing everyone else in the industry, calling them all 'wankers' and making them look incompetent. We needed to make amends and comforting noises. We should have offered to tie ourselves into the industry more, but Pete enjoyed being confrontational. You had to admire his cheek, but the resentment towards us increased. Behind the scenes it was felt that PWL scoring more than 15 Top Ten hits in a year was too much for one small independent record label. On top of that, Pete was trying to push artists onto us that we shouldn't have touched, such as more soap stars, but those who didn't have the same qualities or abilities as Kylie or Jason. Some of them weren't talented at all and people were saying, 'Well, if they make *that* person a hit, they can make anybody a hit.'

Feedback from the public was our guiding force, and they liked our songs so much we gave them more. In a way I agreed with Pete's view of the industry. Most people in the business don't listen to the public, and only want to make records for themselves. I've never made the record that I want to make; I'm sure it would be interesting, but it might not be a hit. We wrote to please fans, not critics, A&R men or the chairman of the board.

It had been years since I had given up playing in bands. My decision to break up Mirage had been sensible, I guess, but it meant spending most of the 1980s locked away in recording studios, working at mixing desks and hammering on keyboards. I suppose if I missed anything from the old days it was the sound of applause and the buzz that only an audience can create.

There were rare occasions when I could get back on stage, however. It's my proud boast that the last two gigs I ever did were at the Royal Albert Hall and Wembley Stadium.

My appearance at the stadium came as the result of the work SAW had been doing with Cliff Richard in 1989. One of Britain's best-loved pop singers, Cliff asked us to come to a special concert to celebrate his 30 years in showbusiness. A few months earlier he'd made a record with us. This in itself was an honour. Along with Tommy Steele, Cliff had been Britain's first rock'n'roll star. He'd had a fantastic run of hit records all the way from *Move It*, *Living Doll*, *Bachelor Boy* and *Summer Holiday* to *Congratulations*, *Devil Woman* and *We Don't Talk Anymore*. But Cliff hadn't always found it easy to slip back into the charts as the decades rolled by and fashions changed. We felt sure we could come up with something suitable. The problem was he wanted to hear demos of our songs and we didn't do demos. As I've said before, why make a shabby version of something? Go for it or don't bother.

We gently persuaded Cliff it would be all right on the day of the session. I would have the song ready, I'd sing it to him and we'd go from there. So, for the first time in his professional life, he didn't hear the song before coming into a studio to make a record. I had listened to a previous hit by Cliff called *Wired For Sound* and pitched our song called *I Just Don't Have The Heart* in the same key. When I sang the tune he said it was too high for him, and when I told him I'd checked with *Wired For Sound* he quickly informed me that *Wired* had been recorded eight years ago and his voice had dropped a bit since then. So I took the song down a tone and he was brilliant. He sang it perfectly in tune very quickly. It was a great experience.

At the end of the session, Cliff asked if he could take a copy of the tape home. That was against our policy – for his own protection we didn't want the song to be heard yet as we hadn't finished putting it into shape. Cliff assured me that that wouldn't be a problem. He said he'd been in the business for 30 years and he knew what he was doing. He also said that he wouldn't play it to anybody. However, when we came to do the final mix he admitted he had played it to his mum and that she had loved it. Even worse – he had played to his milkman. I fell off my stool.

'Why did you play it to the milkman?'

'Oh, I play all of my songs to the milkman. And if he likes it, then I know it will be a hit.'

No harm done, though, as the record became a Top Ten hit. The week it was at Number Three in August 1989 Cliff was in Portugal playing tennis so he couldn't go on *Top Of The Pops*. I'm sure it would have been Number One if he had been there to promote it. Nevertheless, he asked us to perform the song with him at Wembley Stadium.

Cliff also told us something rather disturbing. 'By the way, I've been out on tour around the world and I've never had to defend anybody the way I have you guys. I'm a Christian and I've never had to defend God as much as I've had to defend you.' It seemed the media had attacked Cliff for working with Stock Aitken Waterman. It was our Svengali reputation again. I suppose the way we worked was getting up their noses, but it was precisely as a result of our unique methods that we got the results we did.

I'd written the song with Matt in the studio and hadn't let Cliff hear it until recording day. We just wanted to get the record out and let the public decide if they liked it or not. As it turned out, the public loved it, and I was up there on stage at Wembley Stadium with Sir Cliff playing the keyboards, while Matt played guitar, Pete hit a tambourine and we all sang along with Cliff and his band.

We also did a show at the Royal Albert Hall in 1989. It was a charity event called 'SAW Goes To The Albert', organized by the *Daily Star* newspaper. We got all of our artists to come along and perform, and Matt, Pete and I did *Roadblock*. Pete played tambourine and I played the bass. We made a video and raised several million pounds for the Royal Marsden Hospital Appeal.

It wasn't a bad thing to put on your CV: 'Last two public appearances – Wembley Stadium and the Royal Albert Hall.' On the whole it was a wonderful time.

Stock Aitken Waterman became a trusted, recognized name. The public wanted our product, whoever happened to be singing on our records. As we have seen, the SAW brand name was becoming bigger than the artists. Not as big as long-established individuals like Cliff Richard or Donna Summer, of course, but we were certainly bigger than some of the new acts we were recording. Let's face it, many of them were just unknown kids. People began to assume it was going to be a good pop record if it had Stock Aitken Waterman on the label; they had a lot of faith in that name.

Historically speaking, record producers tended not to be well known. Phil Spector made a name with his 'Wall of Sound' and, of course, everyone knew Sir George Martin who produced The Beatles, but mostly producers were backroom boys. We broke the mould, partly because Pete was so good at promotion.

We were unusual, if not unique. Matt and I wrote, arranged and even played all the music on all the records, and Pete put them out on his own label, and marketed and promoted the records. The decision to promote us as a brand seemed logical, and the brand itself had evolved organically rather than been the product of a conscious decision. We were more punk than punk rock. What we did was unheard of and shook the industry to the core. In the process we took their business away, which they didn't like.

The industry was embarrassed and the parent companies started to ask questions. We could just imagine the chairmen storming into boardrooms and demanding of their quaking staff: 'Why are you allowing market share to go to this upstart independent label?' Meanwhile, Pete was cheerfully rubbing their noses in it. So they got more upset and we got blasted as the puppeteers and Svengalis of pop. Some of the things that were said were incredibly personal and quite nasty, but I learned to treat both criticism and praise with equal disdain and relied instead on my own judgement and self-belief.

There was also a severe backlash from fashion aficionados, who thought *they* were the star-makers. They hated what we did as much as the seething 'majors'. The more we did it, the more they hated us. It became a recurrent theme that *we* were now the pop Establishment. But we weren't.

We started to lose friends and gain enemies in all quarters. We had set out starry-eyed and full of enthusiasm, intending to create a British-style Tamla Motown. Now there was an orchestrated backlash that became aggressive and upset us badly. There was only one thing we could do. Get back to the Hit Factory and create some more chart-busters!

I CAN WRITE YOU A HIT!

As Stock Aitken Waterman unleashed a flow of hits, I'm sure many people thought it was child's play. 'Money for old rope, mate. I could do that standing on me 'ead.' The blokes down the pub all had their theories. So did the critics. Even some of our own artists thought we were churning out records like a human conveyer belt.

But it wasn't that easy. The secret of our success lay in hard work, long hours and those magical 'eureka' moments. Over the years we developed an approach that produced stunning results. Even now it's hard to comprehend how much we achieved. At the time we were caught up in the frenzy of deadlines and demands. We didn't have time to sit back and wonder at how it was all happening. But our instincts told us we were winning, and so did the public.

So, how *do* you write a smash hit? Well, you need inspiration and experience. In our case we also had basic working structures in place. Our success rate didn't happen by accident. We knew exactly what we were doing on each record and, having discussed the artist and the song, we understood the audience we were trying to reach. The first objective was to create a solid musical base. Down at the Hit Factory, Matt and I *were* the band, and the singers were the guest vocalists. The songs were doing the selling and the artists were an adjunct. To put it in perspective: Matt and I played every single instrument on all the SAW hit records. Bar-room experts might like to consider how much effort was put into making so many albums and singles, but I can assure you we didn't get results by ordering another pint of lager and a packet of crisps – even though that might have worked for Max Splodge.*

Of course, technology helped. By the late 1980s we were using 48-track recording facilities and filling virtually every track ourselves. We had help from backing singers, but I often sang the BVs (backing vocals) as well. Matt is an excellent guitarist and keyboard player, and we both programmed drum computers and used brass and string synthesizers. As a result, we played all the instruments on 400 records, and nobody has sung on more hits than me! Once each track was completed, we handed the finished product over to the office to do the promotion.

It was a very tightly controlled operation, and I didn't mind when people said, 'That sounds like a SAW hit.' That was fine by me – I felt it was a seal of approval. And there were stylistic differences between the tracks. During the 1980s we moved from the Hi-NRG of Dead Or Alive to the R&B soul of Princess and the high camp of Bananarama. Later on we moved into house music with Mel & Kim and pure pop with Kylie and Jason.

If public opinion was polarized over a particular song, then I *knew* we had a hit record. If 50 per cent of the population hate a record, then 50 per cent will probably love it. The Beatles went through the same kind of thing. Their records won both criticism and praise. People look back on their albums and regard them as artistic statements, but a lot of it was simple pop music. *I Should Be So Lucky* is no different from *She Loves You* – it's all just youthful bubblegum.

●

When you start to write a pop song you have to consider what route you want to take as there are two distinct kinds of song. There are groove-based themes where a drummer and guitarist get together to create a riff and the singer fits a song into the groove. All the great soul artists sing licks over grooves. Their songs are liberally splattered with ad-lib 'babies' and 'ooh

---

* *Max Splodge, singer with Splodgenessabounds, scored a Number Seven hit with* Two Pints Of Lager And A Packet Of Crisps Please *in June 1980.*

yeahs' that fill gaps and make it rhythmic. We studiously avoided the need to say 'baby' in a song. It's not a phrase that figures in modern everyday English, so why would you sing it? It's only because rhythmically you need to fill a gap. But if you have a structured song you don't need to fill gaps. The highly structured song is the second type.

I always try to write structured songs that don't have holes. Rodgers & Hammerstein's songs from the musicals are some of the finest examples of great pop composition. When I went to the pictures as a kid I used to be quite affected by the old, simple songs sung by Al Jolson. I also liked British music-hall songs, such as *My Dear Old Dutch*, which have simple and honest sentiments expressed in a moving way. They talk about ordinary life and aren't full of americanisms. If you live in London, why pretend you are from New York?

Songs that have resonance are the ones that work for me. I like songs about human relationships. In terms of content, there have really only ever been two songs: one is about being happy and the other is about being sad. My songs tend to be about the search for happiness and celebrate love, life and longing. Longing is a journey we all take. We all wish for something better, we all need a goal to work towards, and a lot of my songs have that idea as their central theme.

Okay, so a hit song needs some emotional depth. If it's going to be any good or stand a chance it's got to strike a chord with people. But where do you start? Most of the time I'd start with a title and that could come from any source. In our case, Pete, Matt or myself came up with ideas. I might spot an item in a newspaper or on television. We used to say to each other all the time: 'That would make a great title for a song.'

Ultimately, pop music is about simple tunes for simple occasions and you shouldn't get overambitious. Sometimes chord sequences can be quite complex and lyrics a bit overwrought.

> **ULTIMATELY, POP MUSIC IS ABOUT SIMPLE TUNES FOR SIMPLE OCCASIONS**

I always simplify a song and bring it down to its purest form. People might think the *Fast Food Song*, which I wrote for the Fast Food Rockers in 2003, was very simple. But to write a verse and a bridge to lead into the silly chorus of the *Fast Food Song* was very difficult.

When a hit record appears in the charts and gets played on the radio it's all in front of you and you can't break down the components. The record becomes part of the ether. It seems as though *I Should Be So Lucky* has always been there, but there was a point when that familiar song didn't exist. I had to sit down and put pen to paper and make that idea into something tangible.

All songs start like that. Everyone thinks they leap into the mind fully formed. They don't. Think of *White Christmas* by Irving Berlin. The first time you hear that song you love it. Now we've all heard it a million times and it's part of our culture. The tune is full of semi-tones that are very difficult to use these days because they sound too 'musical' for modern ears. That tune didn't exist at one point in time, but now we think it has always been there. Sometimes ideas do just arrive from nobody knows where, so perhaps there is a universal pool of music that some people can dive into and pull out tunes from.

I get ideas, but the only way I can express them is by playing them on the keyboard or guitar or by singing to myself; I don't read or write music on a score. I've never had the need or desire to learn. When I'm writing I'm thinking in production terms. My left hand plays the bottom end of the track, the right hand is the middle and my voice represents the singer. It's a kind of on-going arrangement.

Matt and I spent hours working on songs. I'd then sing the result to the artist after defining the tune. Matt and I made the records and Pete sold them. That was how the team worked, although sometimes the edges got blurred.

Often the song titles suggested themselves when you analyzed the needs of the artist. If you were writing for a lovely 19-year-old girl you wouldn't come up with a song like *Bring Your Daughter To The Slaughter*. Great for Iron Maiden, but not exactly Stock Aitken Waterman or Kylie Minogue.

This may not help budding hit-writers out there, but despite having thought long and hard about the process, I still don't know where the idea for a song comes from. It just hits you. That's the one per cent inspiration – the rest is perspiration. When I'm in 'song mode' I'm on the lookout. My antenna is up and I'm listening to what people are saying. I do believe inspiration comes only when you've left the channel open to receive. In the heyday of SAW my antenna was permanently tuned in to the ether.

There was also the added pressure of deadlines: 'Finish this song and get on with the next one.' There were always three or four artists queuing up and waiting to go. At the record plant, people were waiting to print the title of the song on the sleeves and labels. That always came before the manufacture of the single. Label managers would be ringing up and saying 'Can I have it by next Wednesday?' I used to get quite angry and say, 'It'll be ready when it's ready.' I didn't need to be pushed, I was constantly motivated.

Pete never once criticized our songs. To his credit, he let things roll. And why would anybody change the set-up? It only ever went wrong when we tried to take other people's opinions into account. In our creative business you have to be single-minded and almost dictatorial. You could be a different sort of producer and say, 'Oh, let's go into the studio for six months and work with the band,' but I could never do that. My philosophy was: 'Let's get on with it and make a hit record – now!' I also felt a responsibility to spend an artist's money wisely. SAW made the cheapest records going because they made the greatest amount of money and were done in the shortest amount of time.

> **I FELT A RESPONSIBILITY TO SPEND AN ARTIST'S MONEY WISELY**

ABOVE: Our first album with Kylie went multi-platinum and SAW was deluged with awards. Seen here clutching platinum discs at this 1988 party are (left to right) Pete Waterman, Matt Aitken, MD David Howells, myself and SAW's promotions man Tilly Rutherford.

ABOVE: Jason Donovan, seen here with me, my son Matthew and my wife Bobbie. Jason was fun to work with and great company. He now has two children of his own.

ABOVE: The on-screen romance of Kylie and Jason in the television soap Neighbours ensured that Especially For You reached Number One. Despite spending many working hours with them in the studio, I was too engrossed with technicalities to realize they were actually an item in real life.

ABOVE: Kylie Minogue was a true star from day one, and I'm only glad that she wasn't too appalled by our 'welcome' when she first arrived in London, and that she agreed to let me write her many more 'lucky' hits.

ABOVE: *It was a glam night with the stars when Matt and I attended The Young Variety Club Of Great Britain charity awards in 1988. SAW were 'put up for auction' to produce a record by Brother Beyond. Pictured left to right: Rick Astley, Matt Aitken, myself and radio DJ John Sachs, together with guests.*

ABOVE: *A high point of my career was working with Sir Paul McCartney on a charity version of* Ferry 'Cross The Mersey, *which was released in aid of victims of the Hillsborough football stadium disaster of April 1989 when 96 fans died. The record got to Number One. Pictured left to right: engineer Karen Hewitt, Sir Paul McCartney, myself and members of Liverpudlian band The Christians.*

Admittedly, we weren't often working with creative artists, such as Paul McCartney or Elton John, who might demand long hours to polish their *oeuvre*, if you'll pardon the expression. We were there to assist young singers who urgently needed songs in a basic pop format. We'd say to Sonia: 'You don't know anything about the industry and you're not a writer. Not yet anyway. Maybe later. But we are going to make the best record we can with you singing, so let us get on with it.'

In many ways ours is a profligate industry. It wastes time and money. It's possible to spend £500,000 on a video for a band the public doesn't even like. The record company has to get their money back somehow and that's why marketing departments have taken control. And that's also why most videos are now soft porn that has nothing to do with the song. What is the point of all this? A&R departments like spending money. It's all to do with largesse, big spends, long lunches and lots of catering. The producers can hire dancers and models and film their mini-epics – all paid for by the artists, whether they realize it or not. Some 50 per cent of the cost of a video shoot is recoupable from artists' royalties. By the late 1980s it was impossible to get a record in the charts without a video, thanks to the arrival of MTV.

I was never an expert on videos, any more than I am an expert in my field. I still think of myself as a dedicated amateur, as I didn't have any musical training and am completely self-taught. So there's hope for everyone! But I have always retained my zest for music. Making hits is really a process of discovery. I sit at the keyboard for hours writing a song and it always amazes me when the result has the right flavour or emotional content. That's what makes it exciting. In the days of SAW the artist wouldn't get the whole picture until it was finished. It's like making a film. You don't see the whole film when you are acting in your scene.

To begin with I would lay down a chord structure on the keyboard and add a drum pattern at the right tempo. Then Matt and I would work in a bass line. So we'd got chords, bass and drums. That would be enough for the artist to sing the lines to. I was always looking for harmonic progressions and not just cyclical chords. A lot of pop music is built around a riff over C, G and A minor and F, for example. Guitar bands all play exactly the same thing – that chord sequence could sell 150,000 records. I wanted to get away from that because it subjected the singer to the groove and made them irrelevant – it didn't glorify the singer. My songs went somewhere, they were linear as oppose to cyclical, and I always tried to place the singer at the epicentre. When we got it right we sold records by the millions.

I'd sing the artist the chorus line by line and then the verse line by line, and they sang it back to me, line by line. When the artist had gone home, we'd pull it apart and put it back together in the right order. Then Matt and I would add the strings and brass, drums and a million other components. It might seem rather contrived, but how else could we do it?

In the old days an artist would sit at the piano and sing. From the 1950s right up until the late 1970s there would be a studio full of musicians at work making records. You'd hire a pianist, a drummer, a bass player, a guitarist and a 20-piece string orchestra. You might need 40 people and a conductor to make one record. During the 1960s, band recordings were done on multi-track and then the vocalist would come in and sing to the backing track. Frank Sinatra did it differently. He'd 'wax' a single in one session. In his day they'd make a master straight from the studio recording. I believe he did 32 takes of *Come Fly With Me* with a full orchestra before he was satisfied.

The hardest song I ever had to sing 'live' was Nat King Cole's *When I Fall In Love*. It's in D flat and the first note is very low. There is also a long and flowing string introduction that sets up the opening notes. If you don't get that note right, you have to start again. I imagine Cole had to do that many times before he got a clean note. Those artists were better than anyone today, because they *had* to be good. They were specialists in the craft of singing.

But Frank Sinatra didn't write songs, and Nat King Cole only wrote one that we know about: *Nature Boy*, for which he used the pseudonym Nathan

Cane. They worked with specialist songwriters and arrangers. Nowadays everyone wants to be the performer, songwriter and the video director. You can't be that deeply talented in all those areas, even if you are Sir Paul McCartney. If you are Rick Astley, your gift is singing and the possession of a very unusual voice. His voice was astounding, but he also wanted to be a guitarist, drummer, songwriter and producer. All I've ever wanted to be is a songwriter. If the artist was happy to be the singer, then it was the ideal partnership.

Despite all the work we put in for our artists it was very rare to get any positive feedback. On only a couple of occasions can I remember an artist ever saying, 'Thank you for giving me a hit record.' Sonia was one who did, when she went to Number One with her debut single *You'll Never Stop Me Loving You* in June 1989. Sonia had arrived at her hit by knocking on Pete's door when he was doing a radio show up in Liverpool. She pestered Pete for a sound test and he sent her down to me at our London studio. We wrote a song and she was out of the studio after a couple of hours. The process was quite intense. On the Sunday when the chart positions were announced on the radio, Sonia rang me at home to thank me. She was so excited.

'THANK YOU FOR GIVING ME A HIT RECORD.'

Similarly, in 1995 Robson Greene thanked me for his house! His cover of The Righteous Brothers' *Unchained Melody*, which he recorded with Jerome Flynn, his co-star in the TV series *Soldier, Soldier*, and which I produced with BMG records, was unbelievably popular. It went straight in at Number One and stayed there for seven weeks.

Kylie Minogue can now see how much effort we put in on her behalf. At the time it went over her head. I guess the process wasn't very flattering to people's egos. It was 'Just sing that and go.' I felt it was my job to make a Number One record for them. I was taking care of their career better than they could themselves. I took on that responsibility, but it didn't always win me brownie points.

Some of the artists didn't like their records, even though they were hits. They felt they were forced into promoting them. Kylie thought *I Should Be So Lucky* was a cross to bear, which is a shame. So I was hardly likely to get a phone call from her on a Sunday saying, 'Thank you very much for putting me through this!'

●

I guess we could be hard taskmasters. Matt is very intelligent and great fun to be around. Some of his jokes can be quite off-the-wall and Monty Python-esque. However, he wasn't always great with the artists, as he wasn't Mr Diplomat. He could be quite surly and sometimes reduced them to tears. He was usually only joking but that went over their heads. We had plenty of arguments and rows, but I knew how to take Matt and he always made me laugh. Producing records isn't a popularity contest and you can't be diplomatic all the time. There are occasions when you have to be brutal. There were certainly no punches pulled between me, Matt or Pete. But when you are dealing with delicate young girls you've got to be kind. Matt wasn't good at that. He reduced Kylie to tears on a number of occasions just by saying something thoughtless, such as 'Would you like to leave the room now, Kylie? I've got to discuss bass lines with Mike. Go off and make a cup of tea.'

Things like this sounded sarcastic and she was upset. She wanted to be part of the creative team. But when you are concentrating on recording technicalities you don't want anybody else in the room.

Over the years I discovered that many artists didn't really appreciate what we did for them. They thought the songs came out of a cupboard somewhere. They misunderstood and often downplayed what Matt and I achieved in the studio. It was all new to them and they were unaware of the work that went on. It must have seemed like a magic trick when we created a hit.

Rick Astley later turned his back on the whole industry and said he wasn't very keen on the material we did. He was badly advised. Someone should have taken him aside, talked to him very seriously and told him that if he stuck it out a bit longer he'd be made for life. He was pretty much made anyway, because he earned an awful lot of money very quickly, and has, I believe, earned many millions more from royalties over the years. But he turned his back on it all.

> **MANY ARTISTS DIDN'T REALLY APPRECIATE WHAT WE DID FOR THEM**

It upset me when an artist wanted to go elsewhere and do something different. It was taking bread away from my family, because that's what I did for a living. We earned money from writing the songs, but in terms of record sales the artists earned the bulk of the money.

Rick Astley produced half of his first album and wrote half of it. I only did five songs but those five were released as singles while the others weren't. As a result, we became the focus for everything that he didn't want. He is a good writer, but his songs weren't going to be as successful as ours. I had spent a lifetime writing hit songs. Rick and some of our other artists would say: 'You've written these songs – now we wanna write some songs.' It's like saying, 'I can do that.' But you can't. The way to have success in the pop industry is to come up with a great hit song. If it was easy, then everybody would do it.

I remember when Rick had some problems working on his second album, which SAW wasn't originally involved with. Rick was recording at The Workhouse, a studio in the Old Kent Road that we had acquired from Pete Hammond as an adjunct to The Borough studio, and he ran out of time to deliver the album. It seemed that the product lacked any real potential. It also seemed likely that media group BMG would start to impose various penalties for late delivery. When a fire broke out at The Workhouse and, fortuitously for Rick, destroyed all the tapes, BMG extended his deal and SAW was called back in to complete the commitment. Matt and I had to write and produce four new tracks in just two days.

Having a good song is the starting point. Of course, it's also essential that you've got a great singer. In the music business you need a singer, a song and the right business structure. That's how you get hits. I heard Kylie Minogue say on a television interview with Jools Holland that she thought her period with us in the 1980s was all a bit of a dream. All her records with us were hits and she went through a fairly barren period after she left us. What she didn't realize perhaps was that we had our well-oiled team working on her behalf. We needed her input as a vocalist but we didn't need her to help write the songs. As a result she felt excluded from the creative process.

I still don't write songs just for the sake of it. I could strum away on a guitar and sing for myself and enjoy all of that, but if somebody asks me to make a record for release I go into a whole series of analysis. What are we doing? Why are we doing it? Who are we aiming it at? Who is going to sing it? What label is going to release it? Somebody once suggested that I should make my own record but I never did. I never even thought about it. I used to be an artist in my twenties but it's not something I want to do in my fifties.

Okay, so you still want to know how to make a hit. Think before you write. Some records are very topical, such as football songs. If the World Cup is on then why not write around a World Cup theme? Football songs may not be so great, but they can make good records. That's because they're suited to an occasion and capture the flavour of the time.

You must remember to distinguish between a good song and a good record. The latter can't be dressed up with a singer and a pianist. A topical, gimmicky, sound-effect-driven record can be just as appealing as anything else, but it won't have any longevity. I always tried to write good songs.

I accompany myself on a keyboard but I don't sit at it without a starting point in my head. If I did, then I might be able to press the keys, but nothing creative would happen. Before you start, you have to have an idea of where you want to go. I play around on the chords and set up a dance beat. If I was writing a song for Mel & Kim or Kylie Minogue, I wouldn't set up a shuffle rhythm at 100 beats per minute as that probably wouldn't be suitable for the artists. I always have the artist in mind and think about the last record we did together or what I know about them. There is a whole load of thinking and talking before forming ideas at the keyboard. Only when I have the right ingredients do I start mixing them.

On the morning I'm supposed to do a record I wake up with an assimilation of all my ideas ready to put together. Then I sit at the keyboard and work out some chord progressions. I find a tune that hopefully starts low and gradually moves up in intensity and pitch to get to the chorus. I like to start with the chorus in mind. In a pop song the chorus normally provides the title. A good example is Kylie's *Better The Devil You Know*. Ask yourself: what does that title imply? That sparks off the lyrical ideas. The song then takes shape.

You have an introduction, followed by a verse, which sets up the lyrical idea and gets the listener interested. Then you have a bridge, the linking piece which takes you from a verse into the chorus. You repeat all that and by the time you've done two choruses you're ready for the middle eight bars. If it's not a hit by the middle eight, it's never gonna be a hit! If I then decide to bring in an instrumental section it doesn't matter because the song is effectively done and dusted by then. It has to sound comfortable enough that people aren't disrupted by what you've done. You don't stick in a beat from nowhere as people will fall over on the dance floor. On the other hand, you don't want to be too obvious and predictable. It's how you break the rule that's important. It's fun to put in something unexpected and surprise people. But if you break too many rules you end up with a jumble. You've got to keep the framework pretty tight when you're working within a three-minute pop song format.

All musical forms have their framework. It's how you work within the boundaries that are important. The restriction gives rise to the creativity. I would advise anybody doing anything creative to set up your framework carefully. If you are a painter and don't have a frame you might as well daub on the wall. Where does your picture begin and end? If it's a three-minute pop song then you've got to stick to an intro, two verses, three choruses and goodnight! Three choruses, a beginning and an end. You have to be imaginative within this format, otherwise it becomes boring. Some people said that all SAW songs sounded the same. If by that they meant you could recognize the style, it was a compliment. The art was to be creative within the confines of a framework.

I was promoting fun, uplifting, relationship-based songs. They weren't dowdy. And they weren't just happy-go-lucky records. There was always a twist to the story. *I Should Be So Lucky* wasn't a happy song; it was about regret. To me, the fundamentals about writing a song are to put up your title as the bull's eye. It's like playing darts – if you don't put up your target board, you'll throw your ideas at a brick wall and blunt them. You've got to have something to aim at – at least then you'll know if you've missed it.

At Stock Aitken Waterman's peak I had a strict routine and conscientiously adhered to it. At 11am I'd start by laying down the basic track. I remember the day I worked out the tune for Donna Summer's first single with us, *This Time I Know It's For Real*, which got to Number Three in February 1989. Donna was very surprised that day. She was working on a whole album with SAW and this song hadn't existed the night before. She asked me where it had come from. I explained I'd done it that morning. Later on her manager, who was also her husband, told me that she'd been impressed by that.

Because she was a brilliant singer, she embellished and brought to life the tune in a way that didn't need any further help from me. She got behind the microphone and switched on immediately. She knew exactly what she wanted. Donna liked to have the track thinned out so she could hear her voice very clearly; she always wanted the echo and reverb taken off because she was a precise singer and liked a dry sound. With less capable singers I would sometimes feed them echo in the headphones to make it sound bigger and give them confidence. In Donna's case she just wanted to concentrate on the notes. I would sing the lyrics to her and she would sing them back – with brass knobs on.

> **SHE GOT BEHIND THE MICROPHONE AND SWITCHED ON IMMEDIATELY**

At PWL we had a smallish room for putting down the vocals. It was just large enough to play table tennis in after work! The microphone we used for years was a Calrec 'Soundfield'.** It was a big one with four heads inside it, designed for use with orchestras. Hung over the centre of an orchestra it could zoom down to the violin section for a particular passage. We tried other microphones and they all tainted the vocals to some degree. Once we had the vocals on tape using the Calrec, then we could start adding echo or EQ (equalization) if required. We sat behind the mixing desk, and with Donna's vocals playing, Matt and I added the keyboards.

Donna understood the recording process very well and would often be finished by 3pm. That would be the time of day for us to change tape and go on to work with Bananarama.

We never allowed too many people into the studio while we were working, although Donna Summer was always accompanied by her husband/manager. She became a born again Christian in the early 1980s and turned her back on her sexy songs like the 1977 hit *I Feel Love*. It was wrongly reported that Donna had made a comment about AIDS being a punishment from God for homosexual men, which created a big outcry in the gay community and sadly, for a time, affected her career.

** *Calrec 'Soundfield' – a multi-capsule ambisonic studio microphone invented by Michael Gerzon and intended for use with the 'Surround Sound' format. Each microphone costs £5000.*

That happened some years before we worked with her. She came to us for a re-launch. *This Time I Know It's For Real* got to Number Seven on America's Billboard, but if she had been a young teenager when she sang that song in 1989, it would have been Number One for six weeks. I loved working with her because of her all-round ability. Her tuning, pitch, interpretation and microphone technique were brilliant. It took her a few hours in a day to sing a hit, but it took us another three or four days to finish it off.

Donna once refused to sing a song of mine because it was written in the first person. It was called *Breakaway* and was for her album. The lyric she objected to was 'For too long I've been feeling that our love has lost its meaning'. She thought the emotional message was tempting fate. I told her she was being silly and that it was just a song. But she made me rewrite the lyric in the third person: 'For too long she was feeling that her love had lost its meaning'. Then it sounded like she was talking about a friend, which was the only way she'd feel comfortable singing the song. I felt this weakened the song a little, but you sometimes have to compromise with artists of Donna's calibre.

Donna was the best singer I ever worked with. Cliff Richard was brilliant and so was Paul McCartney. You'd expect them to be good. But when working with lesser singers sometimes a song might not work immediately. You then had to make an effort to work out what was going wrong. Very often it's a feel thing – it's all about how you anticipate the beat and push the song along. Many less-qualified singers let the song rule them. You have to grab a tune and drive it. Kylie was good like that, but Jason wasn't.

After Matt and I left the studio at 11pm, the night shift started and the engineers worked on the mix. By the time we arrived the next morning they were waiting for us. So my first task each day was to approve the mix from the night before. Our engineers were experienced and highly talented people in their own right. I might turn the vocals up a bit and check the balances but that would be it. Then we'd go on to work on Bananarama's or Kylie Minogue's next track.

If the track we were producing was for a big label, like Warner Bros, they would hopefully approve the single and go off and make the video. The mixes were delivered on DAT (Digital Audio Tape) and we always gave the record company a whole range of mixes. Vinyl was still going strong then and it was our job to produce the 7- and 12-inch single versions. By the late 1980s most of our records were being released on CDs, but the 7-inch and 12-inch vinyl singles and cassette formats were still in use. Nowadays it's all CD.

At the end of each day at the Hit Factory I went home mulling over the problems I would probably face in the studio the following day. What songs could I create for Cliff Richard, Samantha Fox or Sonia tomorrow? I didn't take my foot off the pedal and I put myself under a lot of pressure for a number of years. We had over 100 Top 40 hits, not including the albums. So I was writing and recording 70 songs a year, including cover versions.

We did albums with all our artists, which resulted in at least 30 platinum albums. Every Kylie Minogue album went multi-platinum. SAW were awarded literally thousands of silver, gold and platinum discs by the music industry. I have so many that I don't have room to display them all. I displayed some at my studio premises at Union Street in south London, which had a large entrance hall: the walls were 30 feet high and they were covered from floor to ceiling with framed discs.

We were getting hits all over the world, so I was also getting discs from Australia, the United States, Brazil and Spain. In the end I put them in storage in the grounds of my Sussex farmhouse. I have a few up in my office because people expect to see them. I'm proud of them. It's not beneath my dignity to display them, it's just that I don't have anywhere large enough. And which ones would you leave out? I may not have had gold taps in my house, but I probably have the world's largest collection of gold discs.

I Can Write You a Hit!

BEHIND THE SCENES

There's very little glamour and glitz behind the scenes in a pop recording studio, but I still find it one of the most exciting places on earth. At the peak of the Hit Factory's output we were producing chart-busting songs on a daily basis, but it wasn't all just the work of Stock Aitken Waterman, as we had behind us a marvellous bunch of technicians and engineers. And, amid the piles of cigarette butts and coffee cups, they helped us create the sounds we could hear in our heads.

When we were struggling for long hours over the mixing desks, watching the clock and ignoring the endless clamour of ringing phones, we needed the support of our hand-picked experts. Much of the joy of creating pop music in those days came from the team effort it involved. The staff that worked tirelessly behind the scenes bolstered our morale when times got tough, and they bounced the ideas around that went into creating the 'wow factor' that sparked a true hit. They also provided the solid professionalism that meant our work flowed without technical hindrance.

Nevertheless, when tension needed to be worked off or a well-earned break was needed, hard-fought ping-pong battles took over in the studio. To let loose on the ping-pong table was one of the few excuses we had to let up on the work. But after much screaming and shouting over a hot mixing desk into the wee small hours, there were times when you just needed to chill out.

SAW were very lucky. Just as we had our enthusiastic girls and guys working for us in the publishing, licensing and promotions department, so we had our extra pairs of hands – and ears – checking and fine tuning the songs as they came on stream. With thousands of hours and miles of tape spinning away, we simply couldn't keep track of every note, beat and nuance. It's fair to say that without the talents of many other individuals we couldn't have realized what SAW ultimately achieved. I for one, relied on the skills of engineers and mixers to pull together some of the records. Although computers do a lot of this work nowadays, back then you had to have your hands physically on the recording desk, moving faders and twiddling the knobs. It's not rocket science but you do need proper training and you have to be good at your job.

●

The seeds of our operation were sown when we left the Marquee Studios in Wardour Street, Soho in Christmas 1984. The Marquee studio was well used, with sessions going on day and night, and as a result the equipment was beginning to suffer a lot of wear and tear. The mixing desk at the Marquee was very old and there were a lot of highly inconvenient breakdowns. It was getting embarrassing. So, when we set up our own studio we ended up poaching a few of the Marquee's staff. We took with us Phil Harding, who had been house engineer at the Marquee. The old studio was invariably the home of hairy rock groups hammering out 12 bar blues, but Phil realized that he preferred what SAW were doing.

WE ENDED UP POACHING A FEW OF THE MARQUEE'S STAFF

Phil became our main engineer at the Vineyard, and he trained a succession of other young engineers, who would sit beside him at the desk and learn their craft. Phil's experience can be heard on so many of our records. For example, we had written *Say I'm Your Number One* and I asked Phil to mix it so that it sounded like a 1985 R&B song called *Genie* by The Brooklyn, Bronx & Queens Band (BB&Q) and produced by Jacques Fred

Petrus. It had a huge sound with lots of bass. Our song was nothing like BB&Q's, but we liked the funky New York sound. Without Phil we couldn't have made that record, which in itself broke down a few musical barriers as it was considered by many to be the first truly British soul record. It could have come out of New York City it was so good.

Phil brought with him Mike Picking. Mike lived in Southend-on-Sea, some 36 miles from London, and he had often found himself being called back to London at 4am to fix a problem at the Marquee. At this point in the early 1980s we were at the dawn of the new digital age and technology was changing very quickly. At the Vineyard we made sure we had the most up-to-date equipment available so Mike wouldn't have to keep driving back to London in the dead of night!

Over the years we had many engineers come through our doors. Phil was great at making club-orientated disco records, but as we enjoyed more pop success we knew we needed more radio-friendly sounding records. So, in 1987 Pete Hammond, who had worked with Musical Youth, Belle Stars and T'Pau, joined us. Pete became our mixer of choice and was an important figure at the Vineyard – he became known as 'Mix Master Pete Hammond. Like me, he had been a musician in a touring band when he was younger and had played bass guitar in a 'beat' group that was signed to Polydor. However, he was also a qualified electronics engineer, as he had started out as a maintenance man at the TMC Studio in London and learned how to be a recording engineer. Pete had co-produced lots of Top 40 hits in the 1970s. Later he bought a half share in The Workhouse Studio in the Old Kent Road where he produced a UK Number One for Paul Young.

As well as the senior, junior and mixing engineers, we had numerous tape operators, as this was the era in which lots of tape was still being used. They were all salaried staff, so it was highly professional set-up. It had to be professional because we were attracting more and more demanding customers, including major record companies who were paying for the studio time used by their artist. At first, while the new studio was being built, we had to use other facilities. One project for EMI, a Tom Watkins' band called Spelt Like This, was undertaken at Ridge Farm studio in Surrey, but we later brought the record to the Vineyard to finish. In a sense we were selling ourselves to the industry, and these were productions that SAW were being asked to make independently. So there was plenty of money coming in to pay for our expanding staff.

Work went on round the clock at the Vineyard but I wanted to go home to my family at night, and so needed an engineer to sit with me during the day. Pete Hammond would do his mixing work at night but wouldn't sit there for the actual recording, which can be very tedious if you can't have much input at that point. I used to sit with engineer Mark McGuire who was very sparky. That attitude was very helpful as you don't want a placid nonentity next to you when you're trying to come up with the goods; you need somebody to keep you going and to keep the session moving. Mark was very good at motivating people, and he was also a very good ping-pong partner!

We also had a terrific Nigerian guy, Boya Olugbo, who we nicknamed Yo Yo, do a lot of work for us, and we employed a mad Australian called Karen Hewitt. Karen came in one day in 1987 when Mark McGuire was away ill, and ended up working for us a lot. Karen was recommended to us and I really enjoyed working with her. Eventually she went back to Australia, but we made a lot of records together and a lot of hits. As a mixer and co-ordinator she was often liable to do something completely wild, especially with the echo units. But often the best production ideas happened by accident.

On a typically busy day I'd be writing a song while the engineer was getting the drum track down. After the singer had done his or her stuff, Matt and I would spend time dressing up the track. Karen would be there during this process, helping us to get the music down and keeping up a steady flow of tea and sandwiches! We also had help from two fantastic backing vocalists Mae McKenna and Miriam Stockley. They had great reputations and were terrific singers. We used them like an artist uses a palette. I could ask them to sing anything, including tight clusters of chords with lots of ninths to get a really interesting sound. The idea would be to dress up the background so the lead singer sounded like a million dollars. Mae and Miriam worked with us from 1986 onwards and they added fantastic vocal pazzazz to our productions.

The work schedule at the Vineyard was often so punishing that people actually suffered nervous breakdowns. I guess we put them under a lot of pressure. But that was only because in the Hit Factory you had to be on top form every day. When we were up against deadlines and working to tight production schedules, it was a case of everybody pitching in, which was great experience for everyone. As a result, a lot of the people who worked with SAW behind the scenes have gone on to become successful writers and producers themselves.

> **IN THE HIT FACTORY YOU HAD TO BE ON TOP FORM EVERY DAY**

During the late 1980s there was a whole bunch of us working flat out. Among them were Gordon Dennis, Peter Day and Julian Gingell. Julian later worked with Barry Stone, who was also a tape operator, and they went on to write and produce the theme music for ITV's *Pop Idol*, as well as working with many other major artists. They both started out as tea boys until Julian began helping out on keyboards. Mike Rose, who has gone on to produce a huge variety of acts, also started work as a tea boy and then progressed to singing backing vocals.

It was great to see these younger staff develop their own careers, although of course a lot of the guys who were of a similar age to Matt, Pete and myself had already cut their teeth in the business.

By 1987, when things were really flying, we put another studio in downstairs and Phil Harding, who later left to work with East 17, used that for his own mixes. There was a lot of work going on in the Vineyard apart from SAW stuff.

We didn't spend all day writing songs in the studio. You had to check out what was happening elsewhere, so I was always listening to other artists and their hits, seeking inspiration and checking out which way the market was heading. We had to keep abreast of what was happening on the wider pop scene, so there was always music being played inside the Hit Factory. Mark McGuire would often come in the morning after a night clubbing and play us the latest record.

There's no denying we would be inspired by other people's sounds, but that was only part of the process of dressing up our own songs. On a few occasions we would try our records out by testing them in clubs first, but only if it was by a new unknown act we weren't certain about. The trouble was we were so busy most of us didn't have time to go clubbing. We just had to get on with the job of making hits. Our sounding board was really the record-buying public. If they didn't buy one of our productions, we soon knew we had made a mistake. But, as I was always listening out for the magic combination of ingredients that made a hit, we rarely made any mistakes.

I would get a line on what the public wanted and needed by hearing what records they were buying. The alternative was to set up a panel and ask people their opinion, but as soon as you do that you kind of box them in. Whereas before they might just accept what they're given, they suddenly need to form an opinion: 'Do I like saxophones? Yes, I like saxophones!' So it becomes a self-fulfilling prophecy – 'It is written that, henceforth, all pop records shall feature saxophones because that's what the public say they like.'

I'd often come equipped with a readymade tune and lyrics. What we were always looking for was an individual sound for each record that we made. In a typical case we would write a song, get the girls to sing it and then get that much down on tape. Then we had to dress the track up to make it sound more interesting. You've only got 10 seconds at the start to make a statement and get potential listeners interested. Then you've got a minute to deliver the first chorus. All those constraints are built into the songs. You are working within a limited framework but in a sense the possibilities are limitless. Fashion accounts for some of the constraints. For example, before 1986 you couldn't use pianos because techno was in and pianos were 'out' and most pop records featured synthesizers. Then, all of a sudden, House Piano became accepted and the piano was back in fashion.

●

As well as the studio staff there were all the office girls in the back room carrying out all the administrative jobs and sorting out travel arrangements for the artists. They were all very helpful and co-operative, and of course it was fun for them to hear all the hit records pouring out at the end of the day. In fact, looking back the whole thing was unbelievable. It could get very hectic on the 'factory' floor, with stars, their managers, PR people, record company bosses together with the SAW production staff yelling and screaming and demanding a hit?

Mercifully the control room was not big enough to accommodate all those people at once. I think we could just about manage the singer and a couple of tape ops. We never really had a mass invasion, but the phones would ring and there were lots of days when the deadlines really got to us. When the pressure was on I had to shut out all distractions in order to deliver finished songs on time – there was certainly no time for ping-pong or trips to the pub. To make matters worse, I could be working on six or more projects at a time. We might spend a couple of hours on one song, put it aside and add backing vocals to another one. The problem was everyone wanted their song delivered yesterday.

Oddly enough the biggest hassles were caused not by the record companies but by the printers who had to prepare the sleeves and labels for the end product. On one occasion they printed the sleeve to a new Kylie Minogue album before we had actually written the songs! The guys at the plant just invented a couple of titles and I had to write the songs to match. There were also times when they printed the sleeve and got the title wrong.

Time was always of the essence. I guess we should have had a big old-fashioned factory clock glaring down on us. But I never really was a clock-watcher. We just got into a routine and slogged on. It was the only way to survive. It was a bit like running the marathon, where you make sure you don't start off at a sprint and exhaust yourself. Pacing yourself was the answer. I'd start work at 11am and finish at 10pm, by which time we were ready to go off to the pub for a quick pint. Then we'd come back and listen to what had been done that day in the studio. I would finally get home at 1am.

> **PEOPLE WOULD CRACK UNDER THE STRAIN**

On occasions we stayed up until the early hours of the morning to finish off an urgent mix, but that would ruin you for the next two days. We wore out quite a few tape ops doing that. People would crack under the strain. I'd be yelling and trying to get a job done, but you had to be strict. Organization was essential. Tapes were our lifeblood and they had to be kept clean and stored properly. The studio had to be kept meticulously tidy. After doing a mix you might have a jungle of wires sprouting across the room, which had to be cleared up. Our tape ops had to be trained to be very efficient in these matters or chaos would ensue.

Phil Harding did a lot of that training because the Marquee, where he had formerly worked, was very much a commercial studio. When different and demanding bands were coming in and setting up every day, you had to be professionally structured. Phil's studios were always very efficiently run and there had to be a routine. If anybody did anything wrong and messed up the routine they would get a severe bollocking. When you are working on so many recordings there are inevitably occasions when tapes get lost. They are precious and highly valuable commodities and much depends upon them. If a tape wasn't properly labelled with the client's name and date of recording, you could waste an entire morning trying to find it.

We never had any blunders with the tapes, although we'd heard stories of engineers accidentally erasing whole albums. The biggest accident we ever had was a tape op tripping over as he came through the control room door and tipping six cups of tea all over the desk. That happened more than once, but we never lost a hit record. The recording desk was precious and the tapes were our lifeblood. Matt used to smoke quite a lot and that was bad for a recording studio because the ash and dust got everywhere.

●

No operation like ours could have been so successful without the tremendous amount of back-up and support that we got. And that was highly important to me personally, being on the front line. Yet I believe David Howells and Pete Waterman disagreed with me about the importance of this sort of structure to the ultimate success of SAW. Matt and I had carefully set up a system, which included the office and studio staff, as we progressed through the 1980s. We had created a perfect organism that yielded a steady harvest of hits. At the peak of our success it was honed to perfection.

A lot of people have wanted to know the secret of Stock Aitken Waterman's success. Some put it down to sheer luck. But as Sir Tim Rice once said to me, 'It is all due to the songs. It is as simple as that.' So SAW had the songs and the organization to deliver them. One minute we were all pulling together, then suddenly in September 1989, it all started falling apart.

It was all going so well and we were so enjoying ourselves, that it really hurt when SAW broke up, because we had put all our lives into the project. I had personally put everything else in my life on hold while we were writing and producing all those hits. Stock Aitken Waterman almost became my family. To see the whole thing broken up on a whim was very hurtful and remains so to this day.

Nothing justified what happened next. But that, I guess, is showbiz.

OPERATIONS SHUT DOWN

Stock Aitken Waterman had been hugely successful for six years, so why would anybody want to rock the boat? Artists were queuing up to record our songs and our creative juices were flowing. It was true that we had run into criticism as our extraordinary grip on the pop charts grew ever stronger, but that was only due to jealousy and resentment. As far as I can see there was no earthly or logical reason for calling a halt to our operations. Yet in September 1989 the first steps were taken that would eventually lead to the break-up of our unique partnership.

The warning shots came when our business affairs manager David Howells announced that he wanted to 'reshape' the Hit Factory. On the face of it, his proposals seemed innocuous and modest. Yet, as it turned out, they would have far-reaching results. The initial reasoning was that over the previous two years PWL had become a seriously big record label. Although we weren't quite in the same league as EMI, Howells wanted to restructure the PWL organization so it would match the operations of the majors. The cosy familiarity of our ad hoc set-up, with its cramped but neighbourly office, was to be put on a more professional footing. All business operations would be based around Howells' office across the way, rather than conveniently situated next door to the recording studio.

After David Howells made his announcement that he would remove the staff to a new building, which I assumed was with Pete's blessing, I knew it would rob the connection that the studio had with the people out selling the product. This was a connection I had set up, encouraged and fostered over the years. The girls who worked with us were not from the music business. As a result, they were not jaded cynics. In fact, they lived and breathed the excitement of what we were doing. From 1985 SAW had grown organically to become incredibly effective.

I thought David was making a great mistake and I kicked up about it big-time. Pete and David thought this was the way forward, but maybe they didn't understand how it all worked. David may have administered the business affairs, but I felt he didn't understand the spark that existed in the creative set-up. Our team had evolved, and now it appeared to be being torn apart at the roots. I told David in no uncertain terms that this move was going to break us up, and I asked him his reasons for doing it, but I didn't get a straight answer. I felt like I was the only person who could see that we weren't a normal record company. I didn't even believe we needed a managing director; we'd have been better off with people with specialist knowledge. Why should PWL change to be run like all the other record companies when they were failing while we were succeeding? Why should we make the same mistakes as everybody else? SAW did things differently – that was the whole point.

> **I FELT LIKE I WAS THE ONLY PERSON WHO COULD SEE THAT WE WEREN'T A NORMAL RECORD COMPANY**

I could play a track to the girls in the office and ask their opinion. That was important interaction as far I was concerned. You can walk into some offices and spot right away when there is something wrong. There might be a bully in charge creating a bad atmosphere, and if that's the case then nothing will work. If it ain't broke, don't break it, but Pete and David seemed determined to bring about change.

However, it may have been the case that their actions were fuelled by things going on behind the scenes to do with finances, which I didn't know about. They clearly felt the need to take action for some reason. I'm sure David didn't realize then how destructive the move would ultimately be, but the very desire to be like one of the big boys meant that SAW would lose the unique character that was the foundation of its very success.

David Howells got his way with most of the changes, although Lucy Anderson insisted on staying put. She wanted to remain close to the writers, being in the publishing side of the business, and she stood her ground. But beyond Lucy, by moving the office staff away from the writers, who were the engine room of SAW, they robbed the writers of their vital support systems.

●

While David was taking over the reins, Pete was increasingly absent, busy doing his own radio and television shows. In the middle of 1990, with the new regime in place, we weren't doing so well, despite having had 15 Top Five entries, including seven Number Ones, in the previous year. Kylie was balking at signing another contract with us, and instead of stars of her calibre coming to the studio, we were getting strange unknown artists from abroad.

Howells realized that money was being spent quicker than the label could earn it. PWL was unable to pay out some of the royalties that were due to its artists, so Pete began looking around for a deal to bail PWL out. Pete was fully back on board now and making his presence felt.

During 1990 some new characters arrived at the studio. At first I didn't know what these guys were there for, though we soon realized that a new label was being formed as an adjunct to PWL Records called Black Diamond. It was importing cheap records from abroad and they weren't even being remixed in our studio – they were finished products. Admittedly one of them was a successful act called 2Unlimited, but it was a Belgian act that had had some success on the Continent. There were 70 singles released on the Black Diamond label in its first year and I soon began to wonder what was going on. All of a sudden we didn't have any space for our own records. It became clear that Pete was watering down SAW's position in PWL, and Matt and I started getting even more worried.

Matt decided to leave in May 1991. The deconstruction had fragmented our energy, and there wasn't the same sense of drive. Matt had become increasingly disillusioned since the changes in 1989. He needed a break after years of working under immense pressure, but he had also reached the point where he couldn't cope with David and Pete's decisions anymore. Matt and I felt increasingly isolated, and as a result Matt had been spending more time racing cars than making records. Pete and I were left together.

I missed Matt. It was true that we'd had our arguments, but they were only about music or Tottenham Hotspur. The passionate arguments that got most hairy were always about what bass line, drum sound and strings to use. As the instigator of a song I always had a notion of how it should sound. I might go out for a meeting and come back to find Matt had changed the whole sound of a track by introducing a new instrument or changing the way an arrangement is played. Suddenly the 'feel' is different. That's when we'd have arguments, but I always won! Whatever the fights, we ended up with a hit record. However, the process did become wearing, and maybe it was one of the things that brought about the end of our working relationship. I began to think that Matt was arguing just to be perverse. It had become a farcical game of 'Oh Yes it Should!' and 'Oh No it Shouldn't!'

SAW WAS BEING SLOWLY BROKEN APART

SAW was being slowly broken apart.

The guys at Black Diamond seemed to be aiming their records at the new drug and dance culture. You overheard them in the office discussing the quality of the latest drugs on the market. I didn't think we should be making records for people taking drugs. Once you start on that, you don't know which way is up any more. What upset me most about this was that Pete didn't stand up to the drug culture. Perhaps he thought it would ruin his credibility as a DJ if he didn't go along with it. David Howells appeared blissfully unaware of the whole thing. Meanwhile, I was stuck in the middle and absolutely hated it.

There was a dark cloud hanging over us. I couldn't get my pop music released any more because people only wanted heavy, ugly groove stuff – mixes with no songs. I wrote just as many songs and made just as many records after Matt had left, but by 1992 it was all dance mixes that were making up the release schedules.

I remember David Howells telling me the studio was a drain on finances. I couldn't understand how he could get it so twisted – it was the studio that was providing us with all the money. Nevertheless, I loyally stayed on with Pete, despite being approached by other promoters, and for a while I enjoyed the freedom I had in the studio without Matt around. I fully intended to turn the problems and the slack records round and get things back to normal. In reality, all that happened was that I trebled my workload. Pete wasn't in the studio, Matt had gone and I was working on my own.

My continued attempts to produce good songs with good artists felt like a losing battle, as I was getting no co-operation from Pete or David. In 1992 I wrote and recorded 70 songs, just as many as I'd done in 1988. But we had only four records released, and none of them was on PWL. 1992 was to be my last full year of collaboration with PWL and Peter Waterman.

I always tried to get on well with my partners in the Hit Factory, but we never went out much as mates, though we did all go out together with our wives and girlfriends on a few occasions. To begin with Matt and I were friends as well as working colleagues, but because we were in each other's pockets all day long it eventually became more of a business relationship. Pete and I would go down the pub after a day's work to catch up on the latest news and gossip. He was good company and we'd always have a bit of a laugh. Bobbie and I went on holiday to Cornwall with Pete and his girlfriend Gaynor one Christmas. We walked on the beach and froze to death, and there was an attempt to be friendly.

I am as competitive as anybody, but Pete had too much personal baggage. There was always an undercurrent of something. He thought the world was unfair and he had an inferiority complex. I think I understood him, though. We had similar ideas in terms of pop music. He often talked to me about a track we were working on – if he agreed with me then Matt thought we were in league together. When you look back at it, it all seems childish, but perhaps it's more that three-way partnerships are always going to be fraught with problems if there's not absolute trust among the individuals.

It was difficult to call Pete a friend because there was always so much else going on. You couldn't tie him down and you'd never get a straight answer. He's not a man who likes to attend to details on anything. He usually gets by on a wing and a prayer and regards himself as a very lucky person. He said things like, 'Stick with me. I'm the luckiest bloke alive.' And in a sense, Matt and me meeting up with Pete proved that was the case. But if somebody said to me, 'Mike – you were so lucky to have all those hits,' I would reply, 'Yes – and I worked *so* hard to achieve them.' They didn't happen by accident. I believe you can have a run of bad luck or misfortune that stops you from doing something, and there may be an element of fate involved. But when you set your mind to achieve something, work hard and get results, that's not luck – that's work and planning.

One day Pete walked into the office hollering how great it was that he'd just got his salary cheque from Warner. I was stunned… and confused. I asked Pete what he was talking about, only to discover that he was now an employee of Warner.

During 1991 PWL was struggling to pay royalties. However, by the time the deal was concluded with Warner, PWL somehow appeared a viable proposition. Pete and David did a deal worth millions, but I knew little about what was happening. All of a sudden the staff were being paid salaries, with Pete himself getting a basic annual salary from Warner of hundreds of thousands of pounds. I only earned if I had a hit. It turned out that Pete had sold 50 per cent of the company to Warner without telling me. However, What Warner got for their money was not just a back catalogue and a pile of imported dance records, most of which were abject rubbish, but also a 50 per cent share in the recordings SAW had already done, although this did not include all the records by Kylie and Jason.

When Pete made the sale to Warner I was asked to take a medical for insurance purposes. It was part of a 'key man clause'. But why would I do that? The deal didn't involve me. Nobody was paying me any money. I refused to take the medical.

They were strange days. After a few years, when Warner weren't getting any new hits, they took the other 50 per cent, voted Pete off the board as a director, took PWL into Warner and changed its name to Coalition. That would carry on until eventually Coalition went under, and then Pete retained the name PWL.

I felt let down by Pete over the sale of PWL to Warner. I thought that, as Stock Aitken Waterman, we shared the ownership of both the writing and the recordings, but Pete disagreed. I had never wanted a share in PWL, only the rights to the recordings. I always believed the ownership of the records remained with the creators thanks to a handshake deal. It was a shock to me when I found out that Pete thought differently. I guess the real reasons for the break-up of SAW were financial, but it was ugly.

There was no real reason why we couldn't have carried on making hits together ad infinitum, except that we were getting bored with each other. We needed a break. And let's face it, the early 1990s was a grey, austere period. The days of jolly pop hits seemed to be over and we faced a gloomy future of grunge.

Once we had had a brilliant system that didn't need corporate stratagems.

Now there were all kinds of machinations going on behind the scenes, machinations I still don't fully understand. But I could see the effect they were having on SAW's reputation and it left me thinking there was not much point in staying around. I went to Pete and asked him to tell me straight what the company was doing.

> **'HAVE WE EVER NOT EARNED MONEY TOGETHER?'**

'Look, Mike, have we ever not earned money together?' he said.

I took this to mean, 'Don't worry, everything will be all right' and decided to stay on.

Then came the final straw. Dead Or Alive came back to work with me and Pete wanted me to co-write songs for them. The original line-up of Dead or Alive had changed, with only Pete Burns and Steve McCoy remaining, and they were not fluent as writers. The suggestion was that Steve McCoy and Pete Burns should take 50 per cent of the writing and publishing royalties and Pete Waterman and I would take the other 50 per cent. In other words, I would be writing virtually 100 per cent of the song and receiving just 25 per cent of its earned royalties. This was clearly unfair. My workload had already trebled since Matt had left; things were becoming impossible.

I called a meeting in Pete's office and suggested I receive 50 per cent of the publishing royalties in these new songs. I suggested that he could have the other 50 per cent and split it between himself and the others. Pete didn't take kindly to this suggestion, stating that he would never be my junior partner, even though that wasn't what I had asked for. I was not prepared to go with anything less than a 50/50 split. The point is that after everyone has been paid their cut, including the artist, there would still be a profit to the record label. I hadn't meant to put Pete down, but it turned into a blazing row, with both of us screaming and shouting. Finally I said to Pete, 'I'll be on my way.'

And SAW was finished. Just like that.

SKULDUGGERY AND MAYHEM

I walked out of Pete Waterman's office on a beautiful autumn day in September 1993. I immediately went to see some properties. After months of frustration I could suddenly see a whole new life opening up ahead of me. Just because SAW had fallen apart there was no way I was going to give up my involvement in the music industry, not after so many years of hard work.

I made my plans and within three months I had bought and transformed a former coffee grinding and packing warehouse – 100 House in The Borough – into a modern, state-of-the-art recording complex, at a cost of £4 million pounds. On the ground floor were the recording studio and programming and editing suite, with offices above that housed the publishing, accounts, press and marketing departments. The studio walls were lined with hundreds and hundreds of gold and silver discs. I was ready for operations by Spring 1994.

Mike Stock had hit the ground running. I was starting my own label, cheerfully called Love This Records. The idea was to recreate the excitement of SAW, the way it had been at the beginning. Lucy Anderson came with me and so did some of the engineers. In fact, I gained most of the old studio staff.

I set about creating our own version of PWL. That was my plan. As 100 House was only about 150 yards away from the old Hit Factory it would be easy for the staff to get to their new workplace. If they could get to The Borough, they could get to my new studio. It would be no different for them if they were ensconced at PWL or Love This Records.

Matt joined me in January 1994. We teamed up for a few years to make a go of it on our own. We were back together again and it was just like the old days. By the middle of 1994 we were open for business, with distribution taken care of by the independent company Pinnacle. As well as the recording studio we also had a dance studio where Scooch, Atomic Kitten, Billie, 911, Lulu and Stephen Gately all rehearsed their dance steps. It was like Hit Factory 2.

The first record we put out was a worldwide hit – a dance cover of the Jim Steinman song *Total Eclipse Of The Heart* sung by Nicki French. We chose to produce a cover as we wanted Love This Records to make a strong initial impact on the market. I no longer felt the need to promulgate myself as a songwriter. I knew I had a lot to learn on the business side, so I played it safe, chose a great song and turned it into a great dance cover, and it worked. By doing a cover you immediately increase your chances of getting airplay.

It reached the Top Five in the UK charts, and Number Two in America in May 1995. Thanks to our production, Nicki found herself hailed as the UK's top new female singing export of 1995. In less than nine months she had sold two million records and *Total Eclipse Of The Heart* was Number One in seven countries around the world, including Australia. The magic was back.

THE MAGIC WAS BACK

It was Nicki's first ever record, although she'd been singing in clubs for some years and was a very experienced performer. Matt and I also wrote and produced her debut album, *Secrets*, which yielded other singles, including *Is There Anybody Out There?*, released on 2 October 1995. Nicki was naturally delighted at her success and she was happy to sing our praises. She said in an interview when the album was released: 'Like every other aspiring pop singer I always hoped that I'd get the chance to make a hit record, so when the opportunity came to work with Mike and Matt, Britain's most successful record producers, I jumped at it. It was a joy to work with Mike and Matt as they have very clear ideas about what they are looking for when working in the recording studio and they come up with some brilliant productions, but at the same time they are very easy to work with. I am very proud of *Secrets*.'

The artists were happy and so, it seemed, was the record-buying public. Love This Records had arrived. At first the industry's reaction was friendly and not at all hostile. Indeed, I was courted by the industry. They wanted me to come in with them, but I wanted to remain an independent. We were selling millions of records on my own label and also in collaboration with the majors, with artists such as Robson & Jerome. Their brilliant cover of the old classic *Unchained Melody* was released in May 1995 and got to Number One. Stock and Aitken looked set to dominate the charts.

•

One of the first phone calls Love This Records received was from Simon Cowell – he wanted us to do a song in association with the children's television show *Power Rangers*, and it was he who later brought Robson & Jerome to us.

Simon Cowell plays the role of Mr Nasty on ITV's *Pop Idol*, but I have known him for years and the truth is he's really Mr Nice – most of the time! Today he is one of the UK's wealthiest celebrity producers. He's a star of the gossip columns and they say he's amassed a £30million fortune.

I first met Simon when he was a young A&R man. He always had an ear and eye for talent and trends. It was Simon who brought Sinitta to SAW in the mid-1980s. Simon was a sharp young Londoner who had started out working at EMI publishing in 1979. He later set up a label called Fanfare together with Iain Burton, which put out some Hit Factory records, including those by Sinitta. When Fanfare went under, Simon went off and put together a label of his own, which didn't work out.

He then got a job at RCA as an A&R man and in 1989 BMG/RCA made him an A&R consultant. He signed acts such as Curiosity Killed The

Cat, Sonia, Five, Power Rangers, Zig & Zag and Robson & Jerome. He came back to me at a time when things were strained with Pete and asked me to do a record for the World Wrestling Federation (WWF). At the time my son Matthew was aged 12 and he was mad keen on television wrestling, so I knew the kids would love it.

I quickly wrote a Top Five hit called *Slam Jam* for the WWF. It wasn't exactly the future of pop but it filled a need at the time. Cowell was in charge of the project for RCA and he was delighted that I could turn things round so efficiently. I then did a WWF album, and, ever since, Simon has popped in and out of my life.

In 1994 I produced Kym Mazelle and Jocelyn Brown for Simon. They were two American divas who sang *No More Tears (Enough Is Enough)*, which was a hit for us. In the same year I also did *Power Rangers* from the kids' television show for Simon, and we had a Top Five hit with that as well. Then he mentioned he was thinking about doing a record with two actors. I said, 'If you are thinking of *Unchained Melody* with Robson & Jerome, we'll do it!'

Our former promotions man at PWL, Tilly Rutherford, had already mentioned to me that the pair were very popular. Simon signed them up, came to see me and we made the record. It was irrelevant whether they could sing or not. We were making records for the public and they were excited about them. Nobody was pretending they were great singers, but they were great actors and personalities. I made the best record we could and they went to Number One. Simon was right about them. We had a massive record and my relationship with BMG grew stronger. Because we'd had such a hit with Robson & Jerome I thought we should do more AOR (adult-orientated rock) material, but with younger boy artists instead.

Working in the studio with Simon could be an eye-opener. He would say the strangest things! When I first met him back in 1984 he had already been in the music industry for a few years. By 1994 he must have been in the biz for at least 12 years. When I recorded *Unchained Melody* with Robson & Jerome I asked Simon to come into the studio to hear the results. I said, 'Sit back, listen and tell me what you think.'

He was nodding away and said, 'Yeah, very good. But … um … what's that noise?'

'What noise, Simon?'

'That noise underneath the vocals.'

'Do you mean the bass drum?'

'Yeah, that kicking noise.'

He didn't know what a bass drum was, which surprised the life out of me. We were in a room full of people and he was making this admission that he didn't know about bass drums, which provide the basic pulse of all pop, rock and dance music. He admitted he wasn't a musician, but really, he absolutely didn't have a clue. Such honesty is probably the reason for his massive success. I suppose he doesn't need to have a clue, because he can recognize talent and knows what makes a hit. But from then on we used to have a joke with him and talk about the 'bish drum' and call all sorts of instruments by the wrong names. He loves what he likes and he knows what he wants to achieve, but he doesn't fully understand how it happens. Simon Cowell may be great at marketing, but he's also someone who doesn't know an A flat from an elephant's bum.

Love This Records were looking strong after the success of Nicki French and Robson & Jerome, but when I started working with another singer, Tatjana, things began to go wrong. Tatjana was a glamorous young girl from Zagreb, Croatia, whom nobody in England had heard of before. My big idea was to do a dance record with her called *Santa Maria*. Tatjana had led a fascinating life. She was based in Rotterdam, having moved there from the former Yugoslavia in 1979. Her homeland would, of course, later be caught up in the devastating civil wars that engulfed the Balkans. But Tatjana had already escaped and made a new life in Holland. After working as a tour guide, she turned to modelling, and also acted in movies and made television commercials before starting her singing career. She released her first single, *Baby Love*, in 1987, and in 1988 had a Top Ten hit in Holland with *Chica Cubana*.

As a result Tatjana had become hot property on the Euro dance scene. By 1993 she was touring South Africa and the Far East. Yet she was still unknown in England. I was sure that if I could get her into the UK dance charts she would cause a sensation. All we needed was to get a groundswell of support in the clubs with a new Stock & Aitken production of *Santa Maria*, which would be released on Love This Records.

That's when I started getting phone calls. I heard from people in the business that people were making negative comments about us. Very quickly the mood soured. All of a sudden I found I had a bunch of enemies.

The trade body for the British record industry, the BPI (British Phonographic Industry), which controlled the charts, said they had detected 'unusual sales patterns'. Our record was selling on Monday and it sold even more on Tuesday. By Saturday it was really going strong. The BPI thought that, because it sold such a lot on Saturday, it was being hyped.

> **THEY HAD DETECTED 'UNUSUAL' SALES PATTERNS**

Meanwhile, I had a meeting with my former accountant Guy Rippon, who told me that board members at the major record companies were talking about the Tatjana record. They didn't know where it had come from or why it was there. Industry sources had told him that the very presence of the Tatjana single was causing concern because they believed the chart was under their absolute control, and they thought it had been hyped into the chart.

It is true you can 'tickle' a record into the charts, but you can't just buy it in. A record has to have natural legs. It has to sell to the public, and this record really was selling. But by Sunday it wasn't in the chart. They'd pulled it.

What could I do? I complained, and the BPI claimed that they'd had reports of a man walking into a shop in Sheffield and asking for 30 copies. When the shopkeeper asked him why he wanted that many he said, 'Well, I'm hyping the record.' It must have been the first time in history that a hyper had announced to the world, 'I'm hyping!' Anybody could ruin a record if it was that easy. My idea was to defy them and to gaily carry on making records.

They pulled my next record out of the Top 40. It was Nicki French's follow-up. It was their chart and they could do what they liked. It was nothing to do with the public's taste. If they decided to pull a record, out it went. Once again they said they didn't like the sales patterns. It was released during Easter week and appeared at Number 41, yet there were 70,000 records available in the shops. We should easily have been in the Top Ten.

I was told there was 'a faulty barcode' on the records. So if someone was buying the record, when it was 'striped through' it wasn't registering. I said, 'Really? That's funny, because I've got my own barcode tester and all of my copies are testing through fine.' But they insisted that the CD and the cassette format weren't reading when they were being bought in the shops. I asked them to make allowances for that in the sales figures, but they wouldn't. Next they said I was breaching chart rules, and my record remained stuck at 41 despite my screaming and shouting.

I threatened to sue the BPI and go to the European Union court of justice, claiming 'abuse of a dominant position', which is against EU legislation. Their attitude was causing me no end of harm, both professionally and financially, and I didn't want to let them get away with it. My first act was to hire John Kennedy, the best music business lawyer available. We put our case together and started to sue the BPI. A front-page story appeared in *Music Week*, the trade paper, announcing my offer of £10,000 to uncover the identity of the person who went into the shop in

Sheffield. I wanted to find out who had deliberately sabotaged my record. Nobody came up with a name. But there was a lot of negative publicity in the media about people hyping records in the charts, which ultimately damaged my reputation.

Then came another bombshell. I got a fax from my lawyer John Kennedy saying he couldn't act for me any more. We'd have to drop the case because he had been offered the chairmanship of Polygram. So I no longer had a lawyer. In the wake of these events, BBC Radio 1 did a special programme on chart hyping and my name and my company's name were blackened on air. Once again it was claimed by the BPI that they had found unusual sales patterns for my record. I was left reeling by this onslaught.

This was followed by a call from the BPI. This time they sounded conciliatory. 'Mike, look, we don't want you to sue us. We don't want a fight. In fact, we quite like you and think you are valid member of the music industry. We think you should drop your action.'

There were a few friendlier phone calls and discussions and I explained I'd be happy just as long as they gave me room to operate. In the meantime I got John Alford, an actor in the television series *London's Burning*, to put out a record. On a Sunday morning I got a call from somebody at the Chart Supervisory Committee who told me the record had gone in at Number Five, but they were going to drop it down to Number 13 on account of its 'unusual sales patterns'. I raged, not least because I didn't know this man who was calling me on my home number.

I called this guy every name under the sun, and the record still went in at Number 13. I needed an appearance on BBC's *Top Of The Pops* to push it up the charts. But *Top Of The Pops* wouldn't touch the record. They took the records that were at Number 11, 14 and 18. But they wouldn't take the one at Number 13, which was mine.

It was grim. I thought long and hard about the situation. I didn't want to dig up the pitch; I just wanted to play football. So I thought it best to drop the case. I just wanted to concentrate on running the label.

In 1997, after four years of struggle against the record industry, I decided to let Love This Records go. It was very sad. After all, I was employing 40 people and they all had families to support and mortgages to pay. The major labels wanted to squash the independent labels so that the industry majors had ultimate power. It was a policy that continued throughout the 1990s. The tentacles of big business spread far and wide. Not only were they controlling TV and radio stations, they were influencing the retailers. In fact, independent record retailers are now irrelevant. The chart compilers only take data from the big multiple-store chains.

The big companies bought shelf space at the beginning of the year, paying up to £200,000,000 to major high-street retailers. That's how the major labels get their shelf space. An independent record producer, such as myself, would have to fight to get on a high-street retailer's shelves. And if you're not on the shelves, you're not in the chart, because the sample is taken from those retailers' data. And you can't get on the shelves unless you are a major.

As a result, the major labels are in charge of media, manufacturing, distribution and retail. They also own the artists, and ultimately they own the charts. They have absolute power. And what have they done with it? Destroyed the music industry. Instead of putting the customers first, they put them last. Absolute power corrupts absolutely.

They got rid of all the small independent retailers and record companies and by 1997 the industry had a dream ticket. They had what they always wanted: 100 per cent market share. Then all of a sudden record sales dropped off. They were down 10 per cent a year. Nobody wanted to buy CDs any more. EMI start thinking about merging with BMG and the industry giants started panicking. Their first reaction was to begin laying off thousands of people.

The fact was the industry had built its own plane. They put their own passengers on board and their own pilots in front. But none of them knew how to fly.

DRAGGED THROUGH THE COURTS

After the golden 1980s, a time of peace and plenty, the 1990s became something of a battleground. I ended up in court defending myself against some major organizations, and the traumas of the mid-to-late 1990s made me wish I'd trained to be a lawyer.

To say that Matt and I were upset by Pete selling PWL and its assets to Warner is to seriously understate the way we actually felt, and the depth of our feelings is hard to put into words. When we joined forces as Stock Aitken Waterman, and agreed to share the fruits of our labour, we were splitting all production royalties equally, and later, when we were producing our own songs we also agreed to share in the writer and publisher income. We were all on the same level.

CBS Records paid for the Dead Or Alive productions, as London Records did for those recorded by Bananarama. Therefore, these record companies owned the recordings. No problem. The productions we created that were released on the PWL Records label were the result of our blood, sweat, toil and experience, and Matt and I believed they were owned jointly by the three of us. The ownership of the copyright in these recordings, we thought, remained with us. No-one had purchased these works from us. Having said that, it is true to say that this was a unique situation; I don't know of any other like it.

We discovered that Pete believed differently. He had sold some recordings we had jointly created and owned to Warner. And some, particularly the Kylie and Jason recordings, were controlled without reference or recompense to Matt and me. We believe this went totally against our agreement. Contrary to the impression given to the music industry of this dispute, we were not arguing against record companies owning recordings per se. We were fighting our former partner because we believed he had broken the agreement we had made. Matt and I felt we had kept our side of the bargain.

As well as this copyright issue, there was a matter of underaccounting of royalties. We took Pete to Court on both aspects of our argument with him, and for six years lawyers and accountants made a lot of money out of all of us. In the end, Matt and I took our barrister's advice and withdrew our legal action. There was no judgement, one way or the other.

In retrospect, we shouldn't have sued, as it turned out we were actually suing the giant conglomerate AOL Time Warner and Pete Waterman. Warner had deep pockets, and I believe they thought they were defending the record companies' rights to ownership of the copyright in recordings, which was never an issue. This was a dispute between three people who had a unique arrangement and working relationship.

There is a lesson I have learned in legal matters which is that the outcome may have nothing to do with what's right or wrong, or what's fair or unfair. Charles Dickens was right when he said that the law is an ass.

●

As a result of his deal with Warner, Pete had some limited success. But in 1996 Warner parted company with Pete and he went independent forming a new partnership with Zomba Records.

The trouble was, Pete didn't realize how important he actually was to Stock Aitken Waterman. All his life he had got by on bluff. His true expertise lay in bringing in new acts and promoting the records with a natural love of pop and a real ear for a hit. Our collaboration was genuine and our success needed no Waterman elaboration. It's tragic that Pete never realized this.

Pete's first real success post-SAW was with Steps, whose debut single *5,6,7,8* was a Top Twenty hit in November 1997. Steps covered some of my songs. The one that established them as a big pop act was one I'd written for Bananarama called *Last Thing On My Mind*. It was a Stock Waterman song, written after Matt had left. They also covered *Better The Devil You Know*, which had been written for Kylie Minogue.

Pete has become a media celebrity – the man who collects old steam engines and tropical fish. He loves public recognition. He's become a household name since being a judge on the ITV talent shows *Pop Idol* and *Popstars: The Rivals*. Mind you, I don't approve of the attitude of some of the judges, and when I was asked to appear on *Pop Idol* I turned it down. I have since watched in frustration as some brilliant kids have been swept aside and discarded by the show and its panel. It's sufficient to say to them, 'You're not what we're looking for.' You don't have to say, 'You're absolute crap and will never be any good, so go away.' Sometimes the stupidity of the music industry beggars belief.

> **SOMETIMES THE STUPIDITY OF THE MUSIC INDUSTRY BEGGARS BELIEF**

Even though I felt Pete betrayed Matt and myself, it is difficult not to like him. We could still have a drink together and get on fine. But on the subject of SAW I sincerely regret and find it hard to forgive his role in ending our long-standing and highly successful working relationship. I feel he acted selfishly. It was a hard lesson for me in the ways of the music industry.

●

Ever since SAW was first set in motion and the hit records began to flow I'd been on a rollercoaster ride of success and excitement. But the battles with Pete and the BPI, and the fate of Love This Records, seemed to start off a chain of destructive events. If the trauma of a long, drawn-out court battle wasn't enough, the ground now seemed to be collapsing under my

Dragged Through the Courts

feet – literally.

My recording studio in The Borough was being damaged by subsidence. During 1996 London Underground engaged in tunnelling work for the new Jubilee line, which went right underneath the studio in Union Street. It was a major project – a cross-town route being forced through under pressure from the government so the new tube line would be ready in time for the opening of the vastly expensive Millennium Dome at Greenwich. The line also had a new interchange station at nearby London Bridge.

We knew we had problems when tiles began falling off the toilet walls and cracks began to develop in the studio, but it took us a while to put two and two together and realize that it was caused by the tunnelling. It was when the whole building began to move that the penny finally dropped. The soundproofing was damaged and the studio couldn't function properly. I had to back-pedal fast, working with lesser-known artists when I couldn't get the big stars to come in.

In 1996 Simon Cowell had asked me to work with an Irish boy band called Westside. They were promptly sued over the name so they changed it to Westlife – and they would become one of the greatest pop success stories of the 1990s. I did a joint-venture contract with BMG with the intention of producing Westlife in 1996. Then London Underground tunnelled under my building and my studio was put out of action.

Westlife had to be produced there and then. The pop industry moves fast and they couldn't wait for me to move my operation to another studio. I had conferences with London Underground with my lawyer present and asked them to pay me off as I couldn't afford to wait for the legal process. At first they thought they might do it and then they refused. By which time the opportunity to work with Westlife had gone.

A lot more money was spent on professionals: solicitors, accountants and technical experts. This was happening at the same time as the case against Pete Waterman, so it was a very difficult time. I had thought my life was music, not fighting court cases.

In 2003 I launched a new label called Better The Devil (BTD) and hoped that this time the music industry would allow me to operate. Oddly enough, none of the people who were around when I launched Love This Records and who once caused me so much grief are still in the industry. They have all moved sideways or left the business altogether.

Perhaps my fate at their hands was down to their jealousy of SAW's success. I seem to have suffered more than anyone from the residue of resentment over the dominance of the Hit Factory. Anybody would think we'd been drug dealers. At one time Stock Aitken Waterman were voted in a magazine as being second to Margaret Thatcher as 'the worst thing about the 1980s'. It's like when Manchester United goes out on the field at Arsenal – they get booed. Everyone knows they are the best side, but English people hate success.

> **ANYBODY WOULD THINK WE'D BEEN DRUG DEALERS**

Sadly, although the record industry has changed enormously since the days of SAW, it hasn't got any better. The main difference is that it is now very much a closed shop and there aren't even many majors left to choose from. They've all been swallowed up. What does this tell you about them and what they're doing wrong? They're doing the opposite of being creative. To make a biological analogy, when a cell divides, life is formed. When it starts to shrink, that's a sign that it's not creating any more.

I suppose the music business should be allowed to shrink now and then, just to catch its breath, but the tendency now is towards more permanent contraction and not expansion. The industry is blaming downloads off the internet for damaging sales, but *they* manufacture the hardware and sell the product and then say how much it's damaging the record industry. If the industry was serious about the effect of downloading it would be relatively easy to stop it. There's anti-downloading technology out there now.

When I criticize the music industry, I don't claim to be a genius, but I can help create acts, artists and records from scratch. When I take them to the majors they should help promote and distribute the records, not involve themselves in the creativity. This is where it goes wrong. They employ A&R Directors who have never been an artist or created a repertoire in their lives. They are and always will be out of touch with the simple power of a three-minute pop song.

Television's *Pop Idol* show is trying to counteract the way the industry has gone. The main thrust of the past few years has been to cold-shoulder plain and simple pop. I make records for people who read the *Sun* and play bingo. Those who run the industry don't have the same mentality; they don't understand what the mass market is all about. They want to impose their tastes on everybody else. They ignore the mass market because it's beneath their dignity. It's pop! It's not supposed to be ironic or tongue-in-cheek or represent an urban lifestyle. Pop is supposed to provide lightweight songs to get you through the day. It's a kind of folk music and is not supposed to teach you anything except how to have a good time.

When in 2003 my new label released a single aimed at kids called *The Fast Food Song*, it sold over 200,000 copies. So despite the impact of Napster and other free music sites, it is still possible to sell physical CDs. The industry complains about songs being downloaded from the internet, but people haven't changed. They still respond to the emotions they have always had and we do them a disservice if we ignore that.

As a hit writer I love the charts and all aspects of pop culture. I know as well as anybody the power of a simple tune. I don't think any of the guys now in charge of our business gets moved by music. They use music as a badge. There is no emotional involvement with it. And these people control what we hear on radio and television and what gets released. It's not just the A&R men who work in record companies who are to blame. It is also the guys who work for the satellite television music stations or for radio stations and the music press. They're all making judgements based on what *they* like. So the airwaves, record stores and the music magazines are packed with their tastes. Their prophecies are always fulfilled. When they predict a record will be a hit, it has to be a hit, because there is no alternative. When you flick the light switch down, the light comes on. That's not clever – that's obvious.

The majors may still be against the indies, but I'm up for the fight. I don't care what other people think. I can still produce pop hits and keep the industry of human happiness very happy indeed!

IT'S ONLY POP BUT I LIKE IT

2004 was the 20th anniversary of SAW's first major hit. After our opening salvo, we went on to become the most successful British record-producing and songwriting partnership of all time – perhaps the world's most successful too. If all our hit singles – and there were more than 100 of them – were released under one name, the lucky group that put them out would have been more successful than The Beatles and bigger than any other act in music history.

When we started out with acts like Divine and Hazell Dean and scored with Dead Or Alive's phenomenal Number One hit *You Spin Me Round (Like a Record)*, it was the start of a decade of chart domination never seen before or since. We had brought to the world's attention such stars as Rick Astley, Jason Donovan, Bananarama, Donna Summer and Kylie Minogue. During those mad, hectic years it seemed like our feet never hit the ground, as if it was all happening by some weird magical process that we didn't fully understand. Peter Waterman says it was luck – I say it was hard work. But whatever it was, it was our foresight and skill that led to the creation of the contemporary pop music scene, which has been dominated more recently by a succession of such latter-day stars as the Spice Girls and Will Young and Gareth Gates.

Our records are still popular all over the world. It's unlikely that there's anybody under the age of 40 who hasn't heard at least one SAW record. We had a profound effect on the course of pop, and yet, as happened to Abba and Tamla Motown, the significance of our contribution was, I feel, never fully recognized at the time.

As the new millennium dawned there came at last a grudging acceptance of the achievements of Stock Aitken Waterman. The dream team of miracle hit writers gained a cult following and our former critics now talk fondly about the 1980s as a golden era for pop music. It's the age-old story: people look back and say how great it all was. At the time they were telling us we were crap.

I have described SAW as rebels who broke with convention, using new production methods and the latest technology. That's partly true, but we were also following in the footsteps of the age-old Tin Pan Alley songwriting tradition. We took time and trouble over our work and based it on years of practical experience in making music. Nowadays any number of Jack the lads working in their bedroom can come up with a decent-sounding product simply by using samples. They amalgamate other people's skills into a collage and put an R&B vocal riff over the top. And they call that songwriting. It's not. It's more like putting together the pieces of a jigsaw puzzle. Some call that a legitimate art form – I wouldn't – but it's still not songwriting.

Of course, we have to recognize changes in the industry. Life never stands still. But the lack of songwriting is now a crisis. British artists aren't getting records into the US charts any more. We get a diet of American music that is streetwise, stylized and heavily marketed, but there's no cross-flow. Yet Middle America is no different from middle anywhere else. If you write a great song it can be a hit all around the world. Everyone responds to a good tune at the most basic human level. Yet the first few years of the new millennium have been the worst ever for UK records in America.

> **IF YOU WRITE A GREAT SONG IT CAN BE A HIT ALL AROUND THE WORLD**

A fundamental shift in attitude is needed. If anyone thinks they've only got to stick in a few heavy rock guitars to appeal to American audiences, they've got it wrong. The Americans have guitars coming out of their ears. They have R&B, soul, country and rock sewn up and tied down. Why should we in Britain want to compete with that? What they absolutely love is British and European pop. Everyone here is trying to give them something they think they might like. What they actually want is pop – done our way. There is no point in sending coals to Newcastle. Donna Summer once asked me why the British tried to sound American. The Beatles might have started out covering R&B, but they were essentially an English pop group.

Back in the 1960s and '70s the US and UK charts were both split 50/50 between British and American hit records. Everyone liked that kind of cross-fertilization. Now, people think we have to make American-sounding records to appeal to the US market. Wrong! All it requires is for our producers to be less blinkered. In pop history there have been some truly innovative record producers. Admittedly, most of them were American. Phil Spector famously created the 'wall of sound' in the early days of multi-track recording, although today it sounds a bit messy. Brian Wilson of the Beach Boys wrote some stunningly brilliant pop songs like *God Only Knows* and *Good Vibrations*. They are still fabulous pieces. Wilson didn't just cycle one system of chords for three minutes, he had a whole load of complex progressions. That grew out of European classical music, whereas Phil Spector came from the much younger American music tradition.

All modern Western music comes from the well-tempered scale of the piano keyboard, which was laid out a few hundred years ago. Even Negro Spirituals and Ragtime came out of that knowledge. It was the interaction between European tradition and American revolutionary ideas that resulted in the whole pop phenomenon. Many of my influences as a kid writing songs in the late 1950s came from America. I listened to records by Elvis Presley and Buddy Holly, as well as the songs from Broadway shows. Yet The Beatles eclipsed them with their fresh ideas and attitude.

I was already composing songs when The Beatles hit the music scene, but they inspired me to start writing in earnest. Paul McCartney, in particular, was a great influence because he was coming up with such great original songs. He was a natural talent who would have happened without The Beatles in some way or another. The others would always have struggled. John Lennon was a rock'n'roller, and that's all right by me, but for me, as a creative songsmith, Paul McCartney was streets ahead. Thanks to Lennon and McCartney all of a sudden it was good to write your own songs and sing with a guitar.

I suppose you could also blame The Beatles for the prevailing view that you are invalid as a performer unless you can both write and sing. I once agreed with that. My view now is that we're missing the point. The greatest singers, such as Elvis Presley and Frank Sinatra, didn't write. Writing is just as much an art as being a great singer.

Theere was a need to write your own material back in the 1960s – if you were a frustrated young kid living on a council estate surrounded by bombsites, you could pull yourself up by your own bootstraps and get out. You could lift yourself up by becoming a footballer like George Best or a pop star like Pete Townsend or John Lennon. Those were the working-class ways out, and pop music became, in more ways than one, an escape. Bands had to come up with their own forms of expression.

Now I think we've moved on from that. Kids now come as fully-fledged artists from the stage schools. They don't cut their fingers in the garage learning how to play guitar any more. They learn to sing using voice coaches and tutors. They don't want to schlep around grotty pubs and clubs when they can appear on television and go straight to the top. There is something in that process but the new breed of pop idols lacks that basic training. The downside is they're not singing about their own experiences. The upside is that there is now greater acceptance that some people are good as songwriters and others are good as performers.

I have no quarrel with young pop stars from the stage schools. How

IF YOU WANT TO BE A POP STAR THE JOURNEY HAS CHANGED could I, when SAW was influential in bringing about that change, and probably even started the movement when it turned television stars such as Kylie and Jason into pop stars. And artists like Will Young and Gareth Gates are bright, intelligent and committed to pop music – they can sing and perform live. I came via the more traditional route of learning to play and sing in the bedroom or garage, forming bands and doing the gig circuit, and I did initially have trouble accepting the way the pop music environment was changing. The traditional route now only leads to the rock world – if you want to be a pop star the journey has changed.

The 1980s was the technological cusp that made what SAW did possible. What we see today is only a natural extension of what happened then. Right up until 1985 there were still bands like all the New Romantics who had their silly outfits and had come together as students at college or school. We changed the scene by taking ordinary working people and making them stars. Then we took television actors and made them pop stars and opened the doors for the whole multi-media phenomenon. The rest of the music industry cottoned on and now everybody cites us a model, in just the same way that we looked at Tamla Motown as our model. The new 'fame school' situation has evolved partly because society is more affluent. You don't have to gig and tour to make money and become a star the hard way. You can study it all at college and go straight onto television and into the charts.

When Stock Aitken Waterman stopped working together it left a gap in the market. Nobody was ever going to fill the gap left by The Beatles, but that didn't mean pop music was going to die. Nothing drastic happened when SAW stopped doing what it was doing, although it was a bad thing when sampling took over. Thankfully there is a move towards people starting to learn to play instruments again. They are going into the studios once more to enjoy the creative process, and not just to recycle other people's work in a cynical and exploitative way.

The music industry is a strange place for any creative artist to work in and it takes a lot of understanding. The uneasy alliance of art and business could confuse even the most experienced artist and hit-maker. There are also the problems of perception, image and marketing.

My biggest problem with Stock Aitken Waterman was that we were stuck on the rails of popular music. Nobody would accept anything else we did. We did *Roadblock* as an exercise in funk, but we had to do that anonymously. Many people look down their noses at the hit-makers – they prefer the unknown artist struggling in obscurity and living in poverty. But what other measure of success is there than to have the public buy your work in vast quantities? I can satisfy my muse as a composer and I know which songs I've written that I especially like. However, I only know I've done it right when a song gets into the chart. It's no good if the public just shrugs their shoulders and turns away.

Since 1991 the British music chart has become a fiction. Yet the record-buying public holds on to its implicit faith in the pop charts as they are broadcast on radio and TV and reported in the press. What the chart does accurately reflect is the records that have gone on display in the big chain stores. You could make the best record in the world, but if it doesn't go on the shelves in a major chain store, then it won't be a hit and will never appear in the chart.

In 1998 Roger Cook, the investigative journalist, asked me to take part in a television programme that was intended to be an exposé of the music industry and the practice of 'chart fixing'. I said I would not personally take part, but I'd give them some help and information. This followed in the wake of attempts by the industry to remove my records from the charts. Cook asked me if I could provide him with a record, which he could then hype and promote to prove his point. So I produced a record and gave him the ammunition to go out and show what was going on. But I didn't want the people I was associated with to be exposed. I told Roger that if they touched certain people whose names came up in their investigations, I wouldn't help *The Cook Report*. I didn't want to 'shop' anybody. I just wanted the music industry to get its act together.

I DIDN'T WANT TO SHOP ANYBODY

Roger got the record into the low end of the chart by using bribery and claimed a victory because there weren't any real sales. We exposed a few minnows, but fell short of tackling the real issues. I don't think the industry liked me for my participation in *The Cook Report*. I created even more enemies.

By the year 2003 British records weren't hits in America or Continental Europe. Bands such as Coldplay have done well abroad, but nobody is much interested in British pop any more. We do have a big local star in Robbie Williams, but he's not an artist who impresses me that much. I have always thought the best quality of any great singer was frailty. For that reason I never really liked Elvis Presley. All that knowingness and hip wiggling, as if to say, 'You know I'm great', was a turn-off. Songs like *Heartbreak Hotel* and *Hound Dog* were classic records, but you could see where he was really at when he started doing *Viva Las Vegas*. It's the same with black rappers who shout how big they are and how great they are; there are no finer feelings involved.

I prefer a singer like Lisa Stansfield, who has a marvellous soul voice and a vulnerable persona. She made a guest appearance on one of our charity records and I would have loved to make more records with her. There were some famous artists I turned down after approaches were made 'through channels'. Diana Ross was one. I felt I couldn't add anything to what she did. It wasn't always about making money – in fact, it never was. I never sat down and counted the money; I didn't even think about it for years, which is why I got ripped off. My sole aim was to make great songs for people. Along the way you acquire lawyers and accountants, but I let them get on with it. All I wanted was to get my head down over a keyboard and come up with a new song.

Among the artists I most enjoyed working with were Mel & Kim, who were a lot of fun, Kylie Minogue, who was a producer's dream because she was so quick and so accurate, Donna Summer, who was the best singer for me because she interpreted my stuff so brilliantly, and Sir Paul McCartney, because that was the achievement of a life-long ambition of mine.

You have got to allow pop records to come through and become natural hits and let the public decide how well they fare. Hit records are the foundations that allow the industry to thrive and in turn provide the resources for all kinds of music to flourish. But the industry isn't very good at knowing what will be a hit. It can tell you how to fake one, but it can't tell you what makes a hit record. If it were up to the music industry they would never have put out *The Birdie Song*. Quite right, you might say, but it was ultimately a big hit. It was truly the people's choice.

Could Stock Aitken Waterman ever re-form and recreate the fantastic success we had in the 1980s? I would have no problem dealing with Pete or Matt again. We still speak and remain friends. If we ever got together again it would be on a specific project. I don't think we could ever reunite and say, 'Let's see what we can do.' No, the Hit Factory could never happen again. In fact, it couldn't happen because the record industry wouldn't allow it. There is less choice than ever now. Even the number of majors is shrinking. There are only five left and there are no independent labels in the charts any more. Some might look like 'indies' but they are really only labels within major companies.

The last decade was quite different from the 1980s. The mood changed. The 1990s was definitely not the age of the entrepreneurial, bleached-blond, bright and cheery 'upwardly mobile' set. Peter Waterman and I pinpointed the date when it all changed as far as we were concerned. It was in March 1990, when the poll tax riots happened in London. It became a different world, all very dark and threatening. Pop music became bleak and drug-orientated. Records were being made solely for people in an Ecstasy-fuelled drug haze. If you were 'straight' none of this made sense.

Whatever people said, Stock Aitken Waterman was never 'Thatcherite'. I don't remember voting for anybody during those years. We were all too busy. We never talked about party politics, but I will admit I was an admirer of Margaret Thatcher, and still am. Politicians today should encourage a positive spirit and a mood of optimism. I thought Stock Aitken Waterman was creating that mood. I thought we could do anything. And the remarkable thing is, with the same concentration and focus, anybody could have done what we did.

BETTER THE DEVIL YOU KNOW

'Can I take your order please – let's eat to the beat!' You could hear the screams of outrage when I launched the Fast Food Rockers' merry ditty Fast Food Song *in the summer of 2003. DJs refused to play it, music critics became seriously disturbed and the press screamed that I was encouraging the deadly sin of gluttony. It all coincided with the outcry over 'obesity', which was blamed on junk food. A song that celebrated the joys of eating hamburgers, hot dogs and pizzas was deemed offensive by our moral guardians.*

While the lyrical content was considered provocative, it seemed people also took exception to the bold simplicity of the song and its innocuous message. The garish and fast-moving video that accompanied the song showed nice, bright, wholesome teenagers dancing and singing a dance number for children. A bouncing beat, bubbly tune and lots of carefully cued catchphrases made the *Fast Food Song* a deep-pan pizza of pure pop.

I knew people in 'the business' would hate it. Yet really it demonstrated all the things I felt had been lost to us in recent years: innocence and fun. The record was only meant to be a silly dance tune, not a social comment, although it had a resonance in today's world. We got many complaints about the video for the *Fast Food Song* video, but most of the videos I see on MTV are gangsta rap songs about guns, drugs, swearing, violence towards women and aggressive prostitution. And they worry about a song about pizzas?

I wrote, produced and put out the *Fast Food Song* by the Fast Food Rockers on BTD. The label was named in honour of Kylie Minogue's *Better The Devil You Know*, a big hit that has been covered by lots of other artists. It's said to be the one song by Kylie that everyone likes; a lot of people found *I Should Be So Lucky* 'too poppy'.

Fast Food Song went to Number Two, sold 200,000 singles in the UK and was a big hit all over the world. It was only kept off the Number One slot by DVD sales of Evanescence, although we were the biggest-selling CD for five weeks. I made the record because I knew there was a market for a vibrant, catchy kids' song. These kids don't want a boring download off the internet; they want to be part of the fun and to hold their own CD in their hands.

My song was intended to plug a huge gap in the market, to appeal directly to kids – not musos – and to give innocent fun a chance to regain a foothold. Our efforts were vindicated by the huge success of the record, and even if the young singers and dancers who took part in the exercise never become Mercury prize-winners, they will be able to look back and say, 'I was on TV. I had a hit record.'

Of course, our main aim was to get a hit record into the charts and generate some cash flow for my new label. At the same time the *Fast Food Song* also represented my desire to take a step back, to get back to basics. I wanted people to realize that pop music should be simple and direct in its appeal. If good pop records make children want to get up and dance then pop can't be such a bad thing. In fact, you could say the *Fast Food Song* was designed to fight obesity and the couch-potato syndrome!

My label used all the latest lines of communication and techniques to make the record. The track was recorded in various London studios and then we went to Oxford to add the vocals and sent it on to Vienna to be mixed. They sent it back down the telephone line and I approved the mixes at my home in Sussex.

WE NEED TO CHEER PEOPLE UP ALL YEAR LONG

The main aim of the BTD label is to make records people want to buy. It's as simple as that! I also like the stuff we do. Within a three-minute format you've got to make something people can dance to that is youthful and relevant. It's not about road accidents or heart disease. It's about uplifting people's spirits. People love Christmas records but we only make them once a year. We need to cheer people up all year long.

ABOVE: *Jason loved being in the studio and wanted to write and play as well as sing. Unfortunately for us, Jason decided he was more into rock than pop and only recorded two albums at the Hit Factory.*

ABOVE: *Sonia was determined to be a pop star and worked incredibly hard. She also brightened up the studio with her bubbly personality and is seen here cheerfully distracting Matt while I concentrate on her latest track.*

EVERYBODY KNOWS
sonia

ABOVE: Sonia's chirpy scouser routine brought her a lot of fans as well as much derision. However, I always found her a very genuine person, and will never forget that she is the only artist to actually thank me for writing her a Number One hit.

ABOVE: Nicki French was one of the first artists I wrote for and produced at Love This Records. Unfortunately, she suffered from the record industry's apparent determination to stop me from having any more hits, but later launched a successful solo career in America.

ABOVE: *Simon Cowell's clients, television heart-throbs Robson Green and Jerome Flynn, became popstars when they recorded a version of* Unchained Melody, *produced by Matt and myself. They had another three Number Ones with us. Seen here at the studio are, from left to right, myself, Jerome, Simon, Robson and Matt.*

ABOVE: *After the break up of the Hit Factory, Matt Aitken came back to work with me at Love This Records. My studio at 100 House in The Borough was not far from the old SAW HQ. At last I had someone to talk footie with again. Here we are seen poised for work in 1995.*

Perhaps the record also represented my own deep need to regain the lost innocence and youthful spirit that had attracted me to the music business in the first place. I had become hardened and cynical after experiencing the pressures that came in the wake of our success with Stock Aitken Waterman. After all, it had been a long haul since the days when I first learned to play the guitar. It was a route that had been taken by so many of my generation, but few had experienced such an intensely demanding and rewarding life as a result.

When I was performing as a solo artist and then played with my own groups I was driven by that need for perfection and the deep-rooted desire to please my audience. I quickly learned the lesson that people like to hear entertaining pop when they are out to enjoy themselves. When I was playing covers I learned how audiences reacted and how classic songs were made. I realized magic could be created in otherwise predictable structures. I noted the tricks of tension and release and those changes in mood that are essential ingredients in any successful pop song. You can't always describe such devices in words, but they become clear when you start putting a tune together on a keyboard or guitar. Even with the jolly *Fast Food Song* you can hear how it subtly shifts from a trampoline beat into something darker, more sultry and sexy in the verse.

The joy of music-making, as much as the need to make a living, sparked and motivated me right from the earliest days. The sound of an audience cheering after a great gig was later supplanted by the thrill of seeing the records I had written and produced storming up the charts. The fact that such records were performed by other people and not by me was not a problem. I'd had my years of touring and gigging. Once Stock Aitken Waterman were up and running I was happy to relinquish the stage for the studio.

Our concept of a 'pop star' began with Elvis and since those early days there have been literally hundreds of artists who could claim that role. Yet only a few became true megastars like Kylie Minogue and few could command the heights of Rick Astley. For every Cliff Richard, Elton John, Paul McCartney or Stevie Wonder, there are many 'wannabes'. They are among the scores of singers and performers who trooped towards the Hit Factory in search of help and sustenance during the 1980s and '90s. Often it was our pleasure to be able to help them get a hit and transform their lives. In fact, there were so many that it's hard now to remember them all. Of course, not everyone who came to us was immediately successful and some weren't suitable for the SAW treatment. We had our share of flops and projects we'd frankly rather forget. Yet I was always quietly satisfied whenever we managed to come up with the goods, even for the most unlikely candidates. By dint of hard work and inspiration we were able to give many complete unknowns a passport to the charts and ensure their holiday in pop heaven.

Some artists decided after their initial success that they didn't need SAW any more, and sadly they invariably fell into decline and disappeared into obscurity. Without the magic generated by the Hit Factory it seemed their star status wasn't sustainable. We needed acts, the raw material for the Hit Factory, but they needed us even more, for our expertise, skill and knack of knowing what the public would like to hear. We could create the songs and the sounds that generated all the excitement. The pretty faces and the vibrant videos were part of the package, but without the songs there wouldn't have been much else to go on. That's where Matt Aitken, Pete Waterman and I held the keys to success.

SAW as a pop music phenomenon was of mutual benefit to everyone, the artists, the public and the industry. Now that the record industry is in such deep trouble and more than ever in need of an influx of new songs and artists, it is strange that they should have so scorned our efforts at the time. But nothing in Britain offends so much as success. We like our Mars probes to crash land, our battles to be lost and our Millenniums Domes to fall into dust. Or do we? I think there is a growing desire in Britain once again to succeed and to be proud of achievement. It is a mood that was encapsulated by the England Rugby Team's outstanding victory in Australia when we won the Rugby World Cup in 2003. It's a kind of confidence, competitive spirit and pride that we also need in the British music industry if we are to survive and continue to prosper. We should no longer accept '*nil point*' in the Eurovision Song Contest.

●

SAW enjoyed a unique position as pop songwriters and it saddens me that songwriting seems to be a dying art today. It's not that nobody else could arrive at the same position as us, as I am sure there are many talented young writers out there. What has changed is that the opportunities for writers have got fewer and fewer. The root cause lies within the industry, as there is no longer the opportunity for anybody to have the sort of breadth of influence SAW had. Radio and television now ensures there is only one musical diet available.

How can a young writer establish himself now? What advice would I give? Just listen. The important thing to remember is that whatever music you like today has a history. You can trace its origins and realize that today's sounds wouldn't be there if the past hadn't gone the way it had. So, to develop a proper understanding of what makes pop music tick, go back and see what route it has taken. Listen to the songs of the past and learn what chords they used and find out how they did things. The onward march of fashion and the changes in tastes mean that much has been discarded or left out. Unless you know what pre-existed, you can't really understand why music is the way it is now. More alarming than the dominance of similar styles is that a lot of dance stuff you hear just isn't music. It may be rhythmic but it's simply a machine-made ugly noise. And unless you are drugged up on Es you just can't stand it!

The best news is that there is now a movement away from hardcore techno and people are looking for songs again. The extraordinary popularity of singer and jazz pianist Jamie Cullum is a good example of a young musician who can sing well, play and write good material. And, wonder of wonders – the public likes him!

A lot of our musical heritage is hidden away. It has become dusty history. All you hear is one kind of music. And why is that? Broadcasters need to get their market share and their audience ratings up, so they only play what they think you want to hear: more of the same. They are preaching to the converted all the time without offering any sort of alternative. There's Classic FM, but if you're a streetwise kid you're unlikely to listen to that. What we need is a radio station that will play everything, like they used to on the BBC Light Programme in the days when listeners could request everything from Toccatta & Fugue to Dave Brubeck and The Beatles. That's the way to get a varied diet of music.

●

I am proud of our hits, but I would love to go back and do them all again! I'm sure I could improve them. In the end we always settled for less than perfection because it was the best we could achieve at the time. The buck stopped with me. I had the final approval on all our records. The mix was normally done overnight and I'd come in in the morning and make a couple of adjustments. When things were flowing the engineers would be tuned in to us and if everything worked out fine there wasn't much more to do.

Most of our work was for PWL, but if it was for another label I would tell Pete when I was happy with it and then he would play it to RCA or whoever. They wouldn't argue with us. At that point, if Stock Aitken Waterman said a record was a hit then it would be a hit. Nobody rejected our stuff because if a production hadn't worked we wouldn't have handed it over. We would have held it back or made excuses and done something else.

The crucial period between a record being released and going into the chart was always a nail-biting time for us, but at the height of SAW's success we were producing so many records our minds weren't always focused on the fate of one in particular. By the time one record was out we were already working on another, so it was a kind of surprise to see it in the charts. You'd let the public decide and see how it all unfolded. Making hits becomes addictive, and we had years of it. A record topping the charts was the cherry on the cake.

Despite all my experience and years of hard work I have to confess that getting a hit record never becomes any simpler. Even during the golden years of the Hit Factory it didn't. In fact, it became harder and harder. But I never lose the thrill of seeing one of my records become a hit, and I'm sure I'll have plenty more. I'm still willing to experiment and take risks. With PWL, Love This and BTD I rarely worked with established artists. I have always preferred the blank canvas approach. When you've got a young singer who has never had a hit before you don't have so much baggage to worry about.

If anybody is attempting to achieve something in the music business today and finds their way blocked by big business, my advice is think and act *locally*. Get *your* bit right. Do a great record. Find out what the public wants and make records for them, not for you. That's the priority. Forget the rest.

POP GOES BACK TO THE FUTURE

Why has pop music been so successful for so many years? Well, it's always been due to a combination of supply and demand. The economics of the business relies on a steady stream of songs and stars to keep an eager record-buying public satisfied. But all sorts of new factors have complicated this simplistic view in recent years. Of course, pop music will continue in some form, but we now face an uncertain, unpredictable future.

For the first time pop faces serious competition from other branches of the entertainment world, such as the internet, DVDs, and computer games, to such an extent that record sales have plunged. It was partly from the desperate need to stimulate the growth of new singing talent that the concept of television's *Pop Idol* contest was born. We can only hope that such 'stars' can last longer than a couple of hits. I'm only too happy to share some of my experience if it will help them survive.

Having spent a lifetime involved in the music industry and seen it from many aspects and angles, I can only say that without the innocence and energy of youth pop music could not exist. It need not be a harsh, cynical business, rather it should be fuelled by aspirations, idealism and hard work. So, despite all I might have to say about shenanigans and pitfalls, those with dreams in their hearts and minds and music in their blood should never give up. And once you have attained your goals there should be enough good vibes around to keep you on track and in the charts.

In the United States there is belated recognition that young and impressionable new artists need help. There is a system of 'mentoring' through which advice and support is offered to young stars from a more experienced person in the industry. It hasn't happened in the UK yet.

Maybe the idea sounds unhip and doesn't exactly fit with the rock'n'roll mantra of living hard and dying young.

We now have a kind of yob mentality in Britain, so an outbreak of common sense probably wouldn't work. But how many established artists, who have survived the excesses of their youth, will wish they had done things differently? Most of them, if they are honest. They might well have appreciated a few wise words along the way. There is no harm in enjoying a fling with a champagne lifestyle, but ultimately it is a wise pop star who decides to look after mind, body, health and finances. It's a good idea to think in terms of the future man or woman, who is relying on their younger self to make the right decisions. Too many artists have come to grief for the industry not to take the matter seriously. In the best spirit of 'mentoring' and at the risk of sounding like a Government health warning, here are my Top Ten Rules for survival in the Great Game of Pop.

1. Don't believe in your own publicity

If you have become successful at a young age, either through a television *Pop Idol*-style show or in the way Stock Aitken Waterman used to create stars, it is worth remembering how you got there. That could be through the hard work of hundreds, possibly thousands of other people. You are the tip of a very big pyramid that includes the people working in retail outlets, record factories and distribution warehouses; there are also the writers, producers, publishers and radio pluggers who promoted you and made the world aware of your existence.

Despite your high profile and glossy image, you are ultimately the end result of the efforts of people you have probably never even met, including the blokes who drive the lorry loads of CDs from the factories to the record stores. You may have top publicists working on your behalf, telling you how attractive you are and what great records you have made, but don't believe *everything* they say!

2. Don't listen to friends in the pub

I have warned against this before, but believe me, 'friends' are not what they seem. They are quick to tell you what you're doing wrong, but let's face it, they don't have a clue what makes a hit record. Do not become 'intelligent' after your first hit and believe you don't need a Stock Aitken Waterman or a Simon Cowell anymore. Galling as it may seem, you can't do it all on your own. Too often, young stars, high on their newfound status, start telling everyone else what to do. I've had that experience with artists many times. A pop idol will announce that henceforth he wants to do heavy rock songs, when everyone around him tries to explain that the public wants him to make simple poppy songs, and it is for those songs that the public love him. In the end the public will turn their back on an artist that changes style too drastically. You should never argue with the reasons that made you successful. Don't change the plot. Don't listen to your mates – listen to the people who buy your records.

3. Don't change producer

Often cracks start to appear in a relationship between artist and producer after only one hit. I never tolerated artists telling me how to produce a record in the studio. I'd just give them the song, get it down on tape and put it out regardless. Later I started to hear comments from record companies or the management. 'Oh, my client thinks he should be making soul records now.' It's always bad news when the artist wants a new image. In these situations I think of a quote from the poet Robbie Burns: 'O would that God the power gi'e us to see ourselves as others see us.'

4. Don't try to be sexy

Kylie Minogue always wanted to be a sex siren when everybody liked her as their cute girl next door. That's not to denigrate her, but so often girl singers feel the need to adopt a raunchy image instead of being nice and normal. There is actually quite a lot of sex appeal in being demure. The Madonna approach doesn't appeal to all.

5. Don't go pole vaulting

Don't do crazy things you wouldn't normally do at your age. In other words when it all starts happening and money starts to pour in, don't go mad and start buying Ferraris, getting married, having children or just chilling out on the beach for six months to drink and smoke. My advice would be to carry on working. Don't stop for anything, because if you go away 'pole vaulting' and come back expecting the public to be waiting, you'll be in for a shock – they will have moved on to somebody else.

6. If you are a British artist, don't pretend to be American

Every singer I know has wanted to be 'big in America'. They think you can only do that by singing in an American accent. You should actually do the opposite: be British and sing with an English accent – the Americans will love that. And don't think you can have a US hit without actually going there. And, if you do go, it will take six months out of your British and European career, which will put you in danger of losing your audience back home. My advice is – don't do it. There is no need to be big in America. You can still have all the hits you want back home in Europe. I've known lots of artists who suddenly disappeared; it turned out they had been off fruitlessly pursuing the American dream.

7. Remember, no journalist is your friend

Journalists are *always* looking for an angle. If they can embarrass, shock or upset you, they will. They can destroy you extremely easily. So never say anything to a journalist unless you are prepared to see it appearing in the *News Of The World*. And keep your private life private – it will help keep you sane.

Among all the stars I have been involved with, Kylie Minogue has largely escaped unscathed the pressures of pop. She has become a real superstar and enjoyed huge success since her days with SAW. Kylie is very good at keeping a shield round her and never lets her guard down. The best policy is to be honest about yourself.

8. Count the pennies

Don't rush out and buy a flash car, and remember that if you spend four weeks in Acapulco making a video, that's your money you're spending. The first thing you should do is buy a house.

9. Watch out for the taxman

Most people who make money quickly soon fall foul of the taxman. Set up two bank accounts. One account for your earnings from royalties, ensuring that at least enough money is there to cover the 40 per cent income-tax liability. The second account should be for personal expenditure. Avoid lots of different accounts.

I think the Inland Revenue should consider pop stars in the same way they view athletes. They allow athletes to spread their income over 15 years because if you are successful in sport you can earn loads of money when you're young but after five or so intense years your athletic career can be over. There is often little difference with the career of a pop star, whose career can sometimes be over within just two years. However, they may have earned £10 million in those two years. It's unfair to take all that money off them, because it's difficult to earn a living over the age of 30 as an ex-pop star.

10. Get yourself an adviser you can trust

However, Rule 11 would be 'DON'T TRUST ANY ADVISER!' The best plan is to take advice but ensure your own financial affairs are in order. Take an interest and don't leave it all to accountants.

But let's face it, no one will ever listen to any of this. I guess you will all have to learn by experience. After all if you are 18 and a pop star, when else can you go crazy and enjoy yourself?

But will there be any pop stars left to benefit from this advice? In the spring of 2004, some 40 years after The Beatles transformed the pop world, there was a seismic shift in the state of the music industry. I'm usually an optimist, but the latest developments cast a gloomy pall over the future. Never before had there been such confusion, apprehension and disarray. During February and March that year came various pronouncements and prognostications from all quarters. One of the most telling news items was the announcement that a major UK high-street retailer would no longer stock CD singles in any of its stores.

Many pundits foretold this was the end of the single, the format that had energized the music world for decades. Since the days of Frank Sinatra and Elvis Presley, the hit single had set the pace, focusing through the excitement of the ever-changing charts. The feverish desire for a Top Ten hit motivated everyone and kept the record industry rolling. At the same time the demise of the single was predicted, top-selling artist George Michael announced he would in future become an internet artist, treating his songs as free music and requesting donations for charity in lieu of royalties. As George stated, he didn't need the stardom or the money anymore. However, at the same time his latest single *Amazing* went into the chart at Number Four and his new album *Patience* was hailed as a smash hit and the best he had released in years.

George Michael's move was indicative of the changes affecting the business. Some saw this as the demise of the traditional way of doing things while others proclaimed it as a golden opportunity for a bright new future. Despite the success of Fast Food Rockers on my own label during 2003, at the start of 2004 I decided to hold off putting out any more records for a while. Amid all the turmoil in the industry, I just couldn't see the way to go. I still maintained a presence in the charts however, thanks to my songs being covered by other people – *This Time I Know It's For Real*, which I originally wrote for Donna Summer, made it into the Top 20 in March 2004 covered by Kelly Llorenna. I guess I'll never stop writing songs. I see myself as a resource, even if the industry doesn't always seem to know how to make best use of me.

Meanwhile, I decided to change tactics. In the past I started labels and waited to see what artists turned up. I only made the records and didn't pick the acts. Artists such as Donna Summer came to me to write and produce her records. I always asked a manager to put a band together or find a singer I could work with. Now I will look for new talent to develop myself. And I will make a success of it.

When I see A&R men at work it seems to me that they haven't a clue what they are doing. They sit behind their desks and make all these decisions, but left to their own devices they wouldn't be able to earn a living. They might work for a big company, but it's all very well being at the front end of a very big rocket when the engines are all behind you – you may feel like you're soaring, but you haven't got a clue where you are going.

What I want now is to find a person who is very talented and highly motivated and make them a star. In the past the only measure for success was having hit records. Now, I don't know whether we are going to be able to measure musical success by chart positions anymore.

With the coming of an internet chart and chain stores pulling out of the market, I want to wait for the dust to settle. There may be other ways of getting music across.

It will be a lot easier if you don't have to physically make records. That will take the distributor and retailer out of the equation immediately. But I hope the public will still want to buy records. It's interesting that some manufacturers have announced that in future they will concentrate on the over-50s market. It seems they are now the only people who go into stores and buy records by jazz or middle-of-the-road artists such as Norah Jones and Jamie Cullum. We have had the rock and pop market for 50 years and suddenly it's all been lost. If young people aren't interested anymore you just have to ask what went wrong?

Pop developed into a big business, but it started out from a love of music and had very small beginnings. The trouble is the industry, as it grew bigger, began to hate the idea of competition. That's because big corporations need to stay big and corporate and don't like individualism. That's why they tried to stop Stock Aitken Waterman when we had such huge success in the 1980s and early '90s and took such a large chunk of their market share. They couldn't stand that. Instead of encouraging us as entrepreneurs who loved music and who had energy and drive, they were very hostile. They fought for absolute power and they pretty much got it. There are very few independent record stores or independent labels anymore. In my view, the 'majors' as well as the retailers helped to destroy the industry.

What we need now is a new pop explosion. We've had many in the past from rock'n'roll to disco, techno, punk and dance music. Guitar rock music is back, but that is a very American phenomenon. The simplest definition of pop is music that crosses over and appeals to all tastes and generations. It could be a black rap record or a boy band hit. If you set out just to make records for one specific age group, for example, then that is 'anti-pop'. You can never completely succeed, but you should try to make records that appeal to a wide range of people. When Boy George became a star it was remarkable how many people warmed to him – even old ladies thought he was graceful and elegant.

But there was no way mums and grannies would have liked SAW artist Divine. When we recorded him that wasn't for a pop cross-over record, it was strictly aimed at the gay community. Divine was outrageous, a pantomime figure, but wacky enough to be successful. There is now a great lack of outrageous pop stars, with the exception of The Darkness. Everyone else is too cool; they have forgotten all about shock, entertainment and showbiz.

Despite those few bands and artists that buck the trend there is no new Elton John and despite claims to the contrary, record sales are generally down. The records first have to be heavily promoted for months prior to release and then they rarely stay at the top for more than one or two weeks. nor do they sell records in anywhere near the quantities SAW records sold in the 1980s. A SAW production by Kylie Minogue sold at the rate of 30,000 a day. Most of her hits sold 500,000 copies and her first single sold at least a million. You don't get those kinds of sales anymore. A record at Number 40 today might only have sold 1,900 copies.

We often see newspaper reports that album sales are booming despite the slump in singles. If The Darkness has a hit CD the media will say 'Album Sales Are Up' because any encouraging signs will be shouted from the rooftops. However, generally the trend is down. If the record industry is in such a state of confusion we must think of the effect of this on the next generation of artists: it must be undermining their confidence.

Yet it may only be those of us in the industry who think all this is so incredibly important, and even I don't know if it really is at the end of the day. Music *is* important, however. It gives people pleasure. But as for the industry itself, which has employed so many people in the past, does its level of importance really matter anymore?

Is there an answer? I think the industry should get behind one big pop chart that simply reflects the biggest-selling records of the week. At the moment there are too many charts for too many genres. It has become ridiculous and produces a kind of segregation not integration. Nobody feels they are part of anything anymore. For example, you are not allowed to have country or classical music in the regular UK chart. Yet once upon a time the chart was a *smorgasbord*, a real mixture of whatever people were buying, so you could promote everyone from Engelbert Humperdinck to Jimi Hendrix.

Unfortunately, hip executives who want 'street cred' control the record industry. Engelbert never had 'street cred' but he made big hit records that dominated the charts for years: *Please Release Me* sold so many copies it was unbelievable. We have lost that aspect of pop music, to the detriment of the industry.

Over the years I have become quite cynical, but I resent what has happened to the pop industry. As a vibrant force it no longer has any real effect. That is because it has been manipulated and controlled for the meanest of reasons that have nothing to do with the music. The loser in the long term is the public and music lover. It is difficult to sit back and watch that destruction going on and remain neutral.

Stock Aitken Waterman revolutionized pop and gave it a tremendous boost. I was very proud to be part of that success story. What we need today is a new philosophy, a new deal and a fresh start. We should be so lucky!

TRACK TITLE	ARTIST	UK CHART
How Do You Know?	Van Dam	unknown
Heartbreak Situation	Andy Paul	unknown
One And Only	Force 10	unknown
Shake It	Rin Tin Tin	unknown
Contract Of The Heart	Spelt Like This	unknown
Stop This Rumour	Spelt Like This	unknown
Anna Maria Elena	Andy Paul	unknown
The Upstroke	Agents Aren't Aeroplanes	81
You Think You're A Man	Divine	16
Whatever I Do (Wherever I Go)	Hazell Dean	4
I'm So Beautiful	Divine	52
Back In My Arms (Once Again)	Hazell Dean	41
You Spin Me Round (Like A Record)	Dead Or Alive	1
No Fool (For Love)	Hazell Dean	41
Lover Come Back To Me	Dead Or Alive	11
In Too Deep	Dead Or Alive	14
Say I'm Your No. 1	Princess	7
My Heart Goes Bang (Get Me To A Doctor)	Dead Or Alive	23
Getting Closer	Haywoode	67
The Heaven I Need	The Three Degrees	42
They Say It's Gonna Rain	Hazell Dean	58
It's A Man's Man's World	Brilliant	58
After The Love Has Gone	Princess	28
Stand Up	Hazell Dean	unknown
I'm The One Who Really Loves You	Austin Howard	unknown
Qu'est-ce Que C'est	Splash	unknown
Samba (Toda Menina Baiana)	Georgie Fame	unknown
Looking Good Diving	Morgan McVey	unknown
Living Legend	Roland Rat	unknown
Love Is War	Brilliant	64
You'd Better Not Fool Around	Haywoode	82
I'll Keep On Loving You	Princess	16
Venus	Bananarama	8 (USA No. 1)
100% Pure Pain	O'Chi Brown	97
Tell Me Tomorrow	Princess	34
Somebody	Brilliant	67
I Can Prove It	Phil Fearon	8
New York Afternoon	Mondo Kane	70
Everlasting Love (Ever Changing World)	Mondo Kane	unknown
More Than Physical	Bananarama	41
Brand New Lover	Dead Or Alive	31
Showin Out (Get Fresh At The Weekend)	Mel and Kim	3

CHART ENTRY DATE	SONGWRITERS	PRODUCERS
unknown	unknown	SA
unknown	unknown	SA
unknown	unknown	SA
unknown	unknown	SA
unknown	unknown	SAW
unknown	unknown	SAW
unknown	SAW/Paul	SA/Paul
02-Jun-84	SAW/Ware	SAW
14-Jul-84	Dean/Miller	SAW
28-Jul-84	SAW	SAW
20-Oct-84	SAW	SAW
3-Nov-84	SAW	SAW
1-Dec-84	Burns/Percy/Coy/Lever	SAW
2-Mar-85	SAW	SAW
20-Apr-85	Burns/Percy/Coy/Lever	SAW
29-Jun-85	Burns/Percy/Coy/Lever	SAW
3-Aug-85	SAW	SAW
21-Sep-85	Burns/Percy/Coy/Lever	SAW
5-Oct-85	SAW	SAW
5-Oct-85	SAW	SAW
12-Oct-85	Delius/Saunders	SAW
19-Oct-85	Brown/Newcombe	SAW
9-Nov-85	SAW	SAW
1986	SAW/Tozzi/Bigazzi	SAW
1986	SAW	SAW
1986	SAW	SAW
1986	Gilberto/Fame	SAW
1986	Morgan/McVey/Ramocon	SAW
1986	SAW/Roland Rat/Meyer	SAW
22-Mar-86	SAW/Glover/Montana/Cauty	SAW
Mar-86	SAW	SAW
19-Apr-86	SAW	SAW
31-May-86	Leeuwen	SAW
Jul-86	SAW	SAW
5-Jul-86	SAW	SAW
2-Aug-86	Glover/Montana/Cauty/Chester	SAW
2-Aug-86	Etoria	SAW
16-Aug-86	Cole	SAW
20-Sept-86	SAW	SAW
16-Aug-86	SAW/Dallin/Fahey/Woodward	SAW
20-Sep-86	Burns/Percy/Coy/Lever	SAW
20-Sep-86	SAW	SAW

TRACK TITLE	ARTIST	UK CHART
In The Heat Of A Passionate Moment	Princess	74
Ain't Nothing But A House Party	Phil Fearon	60
I Just Can't Wait	Mandy Smith	unknown
Positive Reaction	Mandy Smith	unknown
Always Doesn't Mean Forever Every Time	Hazell Dean	unknown
Mind Over Matter	E G Daily	unknown
Whenever You Need Somebody	O'Chi Brown	unknown
Learning To Live (Without Your Love)	O'Chi Brown & Rick Astley	unknown
Hot Mix 2 (Medley)	The Bootleggers	unknown
Something In My House	Dead Or Alive	12
Heartache	Pepsi and Shirley	2
Set On You (B-side of Trick Of The Night)	Bananarama	32
Respectable	Mel and Kim	1
Hooked On Love	Dead Or Alive	69
I Just Can't Wait	Mandy Smith	91
Let It Be	Ferry Aid	1
In Love With Love	Debbie Harry	45
Jack Mix II (Medley)	Mirage	4
Get Ready	Carol Hitchcock	56
Nothing's Gonna Stop Me Now	Samantha Fox	8
Shattered Glass	Laura Branigan	82
I Heard A Rumour	Bananarama	14
F.L.M.	Mel and Kim	7
Toy Boy	Sinitta	4
Roadblock	Stock Aitken Waterman	13
Never Gonna Give You Up	Rick Astley	1 (USA No. 1)
Whatever Makes Our Love Grow	Edwin Starr	98
Love In The First Degree	Bananarama	3
Mr Sleaze	Bananarama & SAW	3
Whenever You Need Somebody	Rick Astley	3
Jack Mix IV (Medley)	Mirage	8
Packjammed (With The Party Posse)	Stock Aitken Waterman	41
When I Fall In Love	Rick Astley	2
My Arms Keep Missing You	Rick Astley	2
G.T.O.	Sinitta	15
Let's Get Together Tonite	Steve Walsh	74
Only The Strong Survive	Precious Wilson	unknown
He's My Boy (B-side of Boys And Girls)	Mandy Smith	unknown
I Just Can't Wait (B-side of Victim Of Pleasure)	Mandy Smith	unknown
SAWMIX I (Medley)	The Hitmasters	unknown
Lock Stock & Barrel (Medley)	Starturn On 45 Pints	unknown
I Can't Help It	Bananarama	20

CHART ENTRY DATE	SONGWRITERS	PRODUCERS
25-Oct-86	SAW	SAW
15-Nov-86	Fisher/Thomas	SAW
1987	SAW	SAW
1987	SAW	SAW
1987	SAW	SAW
1987	Palombi/Jay	SAW
1987	SAW	SAW
1987	SAW	SAW
1987	Various	unknown
10-Jan-87	Burns/Percy/Coy/Lever	SAW
17-Jan-87	Fernando/Fernando/Brown	SAW/Fernando
14-Feb-87	SAW/Dallin/Fahey/Woodward	SAW
7-Mar-87	SAW	SAW
4-Apr-87	Burns/Percy/Coy/Lever	SAW
Apr-87	SAW	SAW
4-Apr-87	Lennon/McCartney	SAW Charity: Zebrugge Ferry Aid
9-May-87	Harry/Stein	SAW
9-May-87	Various	Wright
30-May-87	Robinson	SAW
30-May-87	SAW	SAW
Jul-87	Mitchell/Coe	SAW
11-Jul-87	SAW/Dallin/Fahey/Woodward	SAW
11-Jul-87	SAW	SAW
25-Jul-87	SAW	SAW
25-Jul-87	SAW	SAW
8-Aug-87	SAW	SAW
8-Aug-87	SAW	SAW
10-Oct-87	SAW/Dallin/Fahey/Woodward	SAW
24-Oct-87	SAW/Dallin/Fahey/Woodward	SAW
31-Oct-87	SAW	SAW
7-Nov-87	Various	Wright
12-Dec-87	SAW	SAW
12-Dec-87	Young/Heyman	SAW
12-Dec-87	SAW	SAW
12-Dec-87	SAW	SAW
12-Dec-87	SAW	SAW
1988	Gamble/Huff/Butler	SAW
1988	SAW	SAW
1988	SAW	SAW
1988	SAW/Dallin/Fahey/Woodward	Hitmasters
1988	Various	unknown
9-Jan-88	SAW/Dallin/Fahey/Woodward	SAW

Discography 179

TRACK TITLE	ARTIST	UK CHART
I Should Be So Lucky	Kylie Minogue	1
That's The Way It Is	Mel and Kim	10
Together Forever	Rick Astley	2
Jack Mix VII (Medley)	Mirage	50
Cross My Broken Heart	Sinitta	6
Who's Leaving Who	Hazell Dean	4
I Want You Back	Bananarama	5
Let's All Chant	Pat and Mick	11
All The Way	England World Cup Squad	64
Got To Be Certain	Kylie Minogue	2
Maybe (We Should Call It A Day)	Hazell Dean	15
Push The Beat (Medley)	Mirage	67
The Harder I Try	Brother Beyond	2
The Loco-Motion	Kylie Minogue	2
Nothing Can Divide Us	Jason Donovan	5
It Would Take A Strong Strong Man (B-side to She Wants to Dance With Me)	Rick Astley	6
Turn It Into Love	Hazell Dean	21
I Don't Believe In Miracles	Sinitta	22
Love Truth and Honesty	Bananarama	23
All Of Me	Sabrina	25
Je Ne Sais Pas Pourquoi	Kylie Minogue	2
He Ain't No Competition	Brother Beyond	6
S.S. Paparazzi	Stock Aitken Waterman	68
Success	Sigue Sigue Sputnik	31
Nathan Jones	Bananarama	15
Take Me To Your Heart	Rick Astley	8
Especially For You	Kylie Minogue/Jason Donovan	1
Tell Him I Called	Sequal	145
I Only Wanna Be With You	Samantha Fox	16
Never Gonna Give You Up (B-side to Hold Me in Your Arms)	Rick Astley	10
I'd Rather Jack	The Reynolds Girls	8
This Time I Know It's For Real	Donna Summer	3
Help!	Bananarama & Lananeeneenoonoo	3
Too Many Broken Hearts	Jason Donovan	1
I Haven't Stopped Dancing Yet	Pat and Mick	9
Ferry 'Cross The Mersey	Various	1
If It Makes You Feel Good (B-side to Don't You Want Me Baby?)	Mandy Smith	59
I Don't Wanna Get Hurt	Donna Summer	7
Hand On Your Heart	Kylie Minogue	1
Sealed With A Kiss	Jason Donovan	1
You'll Never Stop Me Loving You	Sonia	1

CHART ENTRY DATE	SONGWRITERS	PRODUCERS
23-Jan-88	SAW	SAW
27-Feb-88	SAW	SAW
27-Feb-88	SAW	SAW
27-Feb-88	Various	Wright
19-Mar-88	SAW	SAW
2-Apr-88	White/Spiro	SAW
9-Apr-88	SAW/Dallin/Fahey/Woodward	SAW
9-Apr-88	Zager/Fields	SAW Charity: Help A London Child
21-May-88	SAW	SAW
14-May-88	SAW	SAW
25-Jun-88	SAW	SAW
2-Jul-88	Various	Wright
30-Jul-88	SAW	SAW Charity: Nordoff Robbins
6-Aug-88	Goffin/King	SAW
10-Sep-88	SAW	SAW
24-Sep-88	SAW	SAW
24-Sep-88	SAW	SAW
24-Sep-88	SAW	SAW
24-Sep-88	SAW/Dallin/Woodward/O'Sullivan	SAW
1-Oct-88	SAW	SAW
22-Oct-88	SAW	SAW
5-Nov-88	SAW	SAW
3-Dec-88	SAW	SAW
19-Nov-88	James/Whitmore/Degville	SAW
19-Nov-88	Caston/Wakefield	SAW
26-Nov-88	SAW	SAW
10-Dec-88	SAW	SAW
1989	SAW	SAW
28-Jan-89	Hawker/Raymonde	SAW
11-Feb-89	SAW	SAW
25-Feb-89	SAW	SAW
25-Feb-89	SAW	SAW
25-Feb-89	Lennon/McCartney	SAW Charity: Comic Relief
4-Mar-89	SAW	SAW
25-Mar-89	Jones	SAW Charity: Help A London Child
20-May-89	Marsden	SAW Charity: Merseyaid
20-May-89	SAW	SAW
27-May-89	SAW	SAW
6-May-89	SAW	SAW
10-Jun-89	Geld/Udell	SAW
24-Jun-89	SAW	SAW

TRACK TITLE	ARTIST	UK CHART
Wouldn't Change A Thing	Kylie Minogue	2
Blame It On The Boogie	Big Fun	4
Just Don't Have The Heart	Cliff Richard	3
Love's About To Change My Heart	Donna Summer	20
More Than Words Can Say (B-side of Love Pains)	Hazell Dean	48
Every Day (I Love You More)	Jason Donovan	2
Can't Forget You	Sonia	17
Never Too Late	Kylie Minogue	4
Can't Shake The Feeling	Big Fun	8
When Love Takes Over You	Donna Summer	72
When You Come Back To Me	Jason Donovan	2
Listen To Your Heart	Sonia	10
Do They Know It's Christmas?	Band Aid II	1
I Should Be So Lucky (B-side of Girls Girls Girls)	Natalie Robb	unknown
Step Back In Time (Mix Back In Time) (Medley)	Rico	unknown
One Love One World	Romi and Jazz	98
One Thing Leads To Another	Yell	81
Ole Ole Ole	L A Mood	78
Make It Easy On Me	Sybil	99
Tears On My Pillow	Kylie Minogue	1
Happenin' All Over Again	Lonnie Gordon	4
Handful Of Promises	Big Fun	21
Hang On To Your Love	Jason Donovan	8
Counting Every Minute	Sonia	16
Use It Up And Wear It Out	Pat and Mick	22
Better The Devil You Know	Kylie Minogue	2
You've Got A Friend	Big Fun and Sonia	14
Another Night	Jason Donovan	18
Hey There Lonely Girl	Big Fun	62
Beyond Your Wildest Dreams	Lonnie Gordon	48
End Of The World	Sonia	18
Rhythm Of The Rain	Jason Donovan	9
Wow Wow Na Na	Grand Plaz	41
I'm Doing Fine	Jason Donovan	22
Step Back In Time	Kylie Minogue	4
If I Have To Stand Alone	Lonnie Gordon	68
Send A Prayer (To Heaven)	Errol Brown	81
Rock The Boat	Delage	63
Better The Devil You Know	Driftwood Overcoats	unknown
Secrets	Sophie Lawrence	unknown
Breakaway	Donna Summer	49
What Do I Have To Do	Kylie Minogue	6

CHART ENTRY DATE	SONGWRITERS	PRODUCERS
5-Aug-89	SAW	SAW
12-Aug-89	Jackson/Krohn/Meyer/Kampschroer/Jackson	SAW
26-Aug-89	SAW	SAW
26-Aug-89	SAW	SAW
26-Aug-89	SAW	SAW
9-Sep-89	SAW	SAW
7-Oct-89	SAW	SAW
4-Nov-89	SAW	SAW
25-Nov-89	SAW	SAW
25-Nov-89	SAW	SAW
9-Dec-89	SAW	SAW
9-Dec-89	SAW	SAW
23-Dec-89	Ure/Geldof	SAW Charity: Band Aid
1990	SAW	unknown
1990	Various	unknown
19-May-90	SAW	SAW
14-Apr-90	SAW	SAW
27-Oct-90	SAW/Aramath/Deva	SAW
4-Aug-90	SAW	SAW
20-Jan-90	Bradford/Lewis	SAW
27-Jan-90	SAW	SAW
17-Mar-90	SAW	SAW
7-Apr-90	SAW	SAW
7-Apr-90	SAW	SAW
14-Apr-90	Brown/Linzer	SAW Charity: Help A London Child
12-May-90	SAW	SAW
23-Jun-90	SAW	SAW Charity: Childline
30-Jun-90	SAW	SAW
4-Aug-90	Carr/Shuman	SAW
11-Aug-90	SAW	SAW
25-Aug-90	Kent/Dee	SAW
1-Sep-90	Gummoe	SAW
8-Sep-90	DJ Crazyhouse/Decarlo/Leka/Frasheur	SAW
27-Oct-90	SAW	SAW
3-Nov-90	SAW	SAW
17-Nov-90	SAW	SAW
15-Dec-90	SAW/Brown	SAW
15-Dec-90	Holmes	SAW
1991	SAW	unknown
1991	SAW	Wright
12-Jan-91	SAW	SAW
2-Feb-91	SAW	SAW

Discography 183

TRACK TITLE	ARTIST	UK CHART
Gimme Some	Pat and Mick	53
Better Off Without You	Hazell Dean	72
R.S.V.P.	Jason Donovan	17
Roadblock '91	SAW feat. Einstein	100
The Concrete Megamix	Pat and Mick	90
All Mixed Up	The Twins	77
Shocked	Kylie Minogue	6
That's What Love Can Do	Boy Krazy	77
The Lucky 7 Megamix	UK Mixmasters	43
Happy Together	Jason Donovan	10
Word Is Out	Kylie Minogue	16
Make This A Special Night	The Cool Notes	86
If You Were With Me Now	Kylie M & Keith Washington	4
Keep On Pumpin' It	The Visionmasters feat. Kylie Minogue	49
Magic's Back	Malcolm McLaren feat. Alison Limerick	42
Say I'm Your No 1	Victoria Miles	unknown
I Should Be So Lucky	Lisa Abbott	unknown
All You Have To Do	Boy Krazy	91
Give Me Just A Little More Time	Kylie Minogue	2
Shake Your Groove Thing	Pat and Mick	80
Finer Feelings	Kylie Minogue	11
If You Belonged To Me	Nancy Davis	86
Step Back In Time (B-side of Summer Song)	Bedazzled	73
What Kind Of Fool (Heard All That Before)	Kylie Minogue	14
Movin' On	Bananarama	24
Summer Holiday	Fat Slags	78
Last Thing On My Mind	Bananarama	71
Celebration	Kylie Minogue	20
Did I Say Ti Amo	Fresh	82
Slam Jam	W.W.F.	4
The Devil And The Deep Blue Sea	Erik	unknown
The Love I Lost	West End feat. Sybil	3
Slam Jam	W.W.F.	75
When I'm Good And Ready	Sybil	5
More More More	Bananarama	24
One Voice	Bill Tarmey	16
Wrestlemania	W.W.F.	14
Looks Like I'm In Love Again	Key West feat. Erik	46
Hot Hot Hot	Pat and Mick	47
U.S.A.	W.W.F. feat. Hacksaw Jim Duggan	71
Energize	Slamm	57
Free To Love Again	Suzette Charles	58

CHART ENTRY DATE	SONGWRITERS	PRODUCERS
23-Mar-91	Casey/Finch	SAW Charity: Help A London Child
23-Mar-91	SAW	SAW
18-May-91	SAW	SAW
Jun-91	SAW	SAW
1-Jun-91	Various	SAW Charity: Help A London Child
1-Jun-91	SAW	SAW
1-Jun-91	SAW	SAW
6-Jul-91	SAW	SAW Re-release
27-Jul-91	SAW/Goffin/King	UK Mixmasters
24-Aug-91	Gordon/Bonner	SAW
7-Sept-91	SW	SW
5-Oct-91	SW	SW
2-Nov-91	SW/Minogue/Washington	SW
30-Nov-91	SW	SW
21-Dec-91	SW/McLaren	SW
1992	SAW	Tommy D
1992	SAW	unknown
25-Jan-92	SW	SW
25-Jan-92	Wayne/Dunbar	SW
25-Apr-92	Fekaris/Perren	SW Charity: Help A London Child
25-Apr-92	SW	SW
2-May-92	SW	SW
4-Jul-92	SAW	unknown
22-Aug-92	SW	SW
29-Aug-92	SW/Dallin/Woodward	SW
5-Sept-92	Welch/Bennett	SW
28-Nov-92	SW/Dallin/Woodward	SW
28-Nov-92	Bell/Taylor	SW/Harding/Curnow
12-Dec-92	SW	SW
12-Dec-92	SW/WWF	SW
1993	SW	SW
16-Jan-93	Gamble/Huff	SW
13-Feb-93	SW/WWF	SW
20-Mar-93	SW	SW
20-Mar-93	SW/Diamond/Dallin/Woodward	SW
3-Apr-93	Manilow	SW
3-Apr-93	SW/WWF	SW
10-Apr-93	Hewson	SW
15-May-93	Cassell	SW Charity: Help A London Child
10-Jul-93	SW/Ford/WWF	SW
17-Jul-93	SW	SW
21-Aug-93	SW	SW

Discography 185

TRACK TITLE	ARTIST	UK CHART
Beyond Your Wildest Dreams	Sybil	41
Never Gonna Give You Up	FKW	48
Stronger Together	Sybil	41
Virginia Plain	Slamm	60
Didn't See The Signs (B-side of My Love is Guaranteed)	Sybil	48
Never Gonna Give You Up (B-side of Seize the Day)	FKW	45
I Believe In You	Kutting Edge	77
Never Gonna Give You Up (B-side of This is the Way)	FKW	63
Beggin' To Be Written	Worlds Apart	29
No More Tears (Enough Is Enough)	Kym Mazelle and Jocelyn Brown	13
Young Girl	Darren Day	42
Gimme All Your Lovin'	Kym Mazelle and Jocelyn Brown	22
Total Eclipse Of The Heart	Nicki French	54
Free Spirit	Kim Appleby	51
Sky High	Newton	78
Power Rangers	Power Rangers	3
When I'm Cleaning Windows (Turned Out Nice Again)	2 In A Tent	25
Total Eclipse Of The Heart	Nicki French	5
Do You Wanna Party?	DJ Scott feat. Lorna B	36
Power Rangers	Power Rangers	57
No Turning Back	Jayne Collins	91
Power Rangers	Power Rangers	65
Power Rangers	Power Rangers	74
Sweet Dreams	DJ Scott feat. Lorna B	37
For All We Know	Nicki French	42
Sky High	Newton	56
Unchained Melody	Robson and Jerome	1
White Cliffs Of Dover	Robson and Jerome	1
Did You Ever Really Love Me?	Nicki French	55
Sleeping In My Car	Mobius Loop feat. Julie Zee	84
Santa Maria	Tatjana	Pulled
Here I Go Again	BND	76
Is There Anybody Out There?	Nicki French	83
Unchained Melody	Robson and Jerome	63
White Cliffs Of Dover	Robson and Jerome	63
I Believe	Robson and Jerome	1
Up On The Roof	Robson and Jerome	1
Eye Of The Tiger	Frank Bruno	28
Beethoven Was Black	Club Risque	unknown
You Can Do Magic	The Mojams feat. Debbie Currie	unknown
When I'm Cleaning Windows (Turned Out Nice Again)	2 In A Tent	62
Smoke Gets In Your Eyes	John Alford	13

CHART ENTRY DATE	SONGWRITERS	PRODUCERS
26-Jun-93	SAW	SAW
2-Oct-93	SAW	A Conte
11-Sep-93	SW	SW
23-Oct-93	Ferry	SW
11-Dec-93	SW	SW
11-Dec-93	SAW	A Conte
1994	SW	SW
4-Jun-94	SAW	A Conte
4-Jun-94	Leeson/Vale/Brisbon/McCoy	SA (re-work)
11-Jun-94	Jabara/Roberts	SA
8-Oct-94	Fuller	SA
8-Oct-94	Gibbons/Hill/Beard	SA
15-Oct-94	Steinman	SA
12-Nov-94	SA/Appleby	SA
19-Nov-94	Scott/Dyer	SA
17-Dec-94	SA/Saban/Levy	SA
17-Dec-94	SA/Various	SA
14-Jan-95	Steinman	SA
28-Jan-95	SA/Robertson/Robertson/Heatlie	SA
25-Feb-95	SA/Saban/Levy	SA
11-Mar-91	SA	SA
25-Mar-95	SA/Saban/Levy	SA
8-Apr-95	SA/Saban/Levy	SA
1-Apr-95	Lennox/Stewart	SA
22-Apr-95	Karlin/Wilson/James	SA
15-Jul-95	Scott/Dyer	SA
20-May-95	North	SA
20-May-95	Burton/Kent	SA
15-Jul-95	SA	SA
15-Jul-95	Per Hakan Gessle	SA
16-Sep-92	SA/Roesnes/Johansen	SA
23-Sep-95	Saunders/Prescott	SA
7-Oct-95	SA	SA
4-Nov-95	North/Zaret	SA
4-Nov-95	Burton/Kent	SA
11-Nov-95	Drake/Graham/Shirl/Stillman	SA
11-Nov-95	Goffin/King	SA
23-Dec-95	Sullivan/Peterik	SA
1996	Bolland/Bolland/White	SA
1996	Linzer	SA
6-Jan-96	SA/Various	SA
17-Feb-96	Kern	SA

TRACK TITLE	ARTIST	UK CHART
Blue Moon	John Alford	9
Summer Holiday	Darren Day	17
No Surrender	Deuce	29
Santa Maria	Tatjana	40
What Becomes Of The Broken Hearted	Robson and Jerome	1
You'll Never Walk Alone	Robson and Jerome	1
Because You Loved Me	Suzann Rye	82
Saturday Night	Sindy	70
If	John Alford	24
Keep On Running	John Alford	24
The Boys Are Back In Town	The Gladiators	70
Don't Cry For Me Argentina	The Mike Flowers Pops	30
Showin' Out (Get Fresh At The Weekend)	Cinnamon	unknown
Casanova	Ultimate Kaos	24
When I'm Good And Ready	Sybil	66
Glasgow Rangers a/k/a Give Us The Ten	The Broxi	54
Better The Devil You Know	Kia	unknown
Love In The First Degree	Sushi	unknown
How Could He Do This To Me?	Tammy Haywood	unknown
Showin' Out (Get Fresh At The Weekend)	Tammy Haywood	unknown
Santa Maria	DJ Milano feat. Samantha Fox	31
Last Thing On My Mind	Steps	6
Ridin' High	Tracy Shaw	78
Happenin' All Over Again	Tracy Shaw	46
Casanova	Ultimate Kaos	29
Especially For You	Denise and Johnny	3
Better The Devil You Know	Steps	4
Especially For You	Denise and Johnny	53
That's What Love Can Do	Toutes Les Filles	44
When My Baby	Scooch	29
More Than I Needed To Know	Scooch	5
The Best Is Yet To Come	Scooch	12
The Best Is Yet To Come	Scooch	64
For Sure	Scooch	15
Airhead	Girls @ Play	18
Respectable	Girls @ Play	29
Lovetrain	Lovetrain	unknown
Fast Food Song	Fast Food Rockers	2
Say Cheese (Smile Please)	Fast Food Rockers	10
I Love Christmas	Fast Food Rockers	25
This Time I Know It's For Real	Kelly Llorenna	14

CHART ENTRY DATE	SONGWRITERS	PRODUCERS
25-May-96	Rodgers/Hart	SA
8-Jun-96	Welch/Bennett	SA
29-Jun-96	SA/Watkins	SA
21-Sep-96	SA/Roesnes/Johansen	SA
9-Nov-96	Riser/Dean/Weatherspoon	SA
9-Nov-96	Rogers/Hammerstein II	SA
9-Nov-96	Warren	SA
5-Oct-96	Riva/Pignagnoli	SA
23-Nov-96	Gates	SA
23-Nov-96	Edwards	SA
30-Nov-96	Lynott	SA
28-Dec-96	Lloyd-Webber/Rice	SA
1997	SAW	Norris
8-Mar-97	Calloway/Calloway	SA Charity: Dance Aid
8-Mar-97	SW	SW
4-Oct-97	SA/Martin	SA
1998	SAW	Norris
1998	SAW/Dallin/Fahey/Woodward	Springate
1998	SAW	Norris
1998	SAW	unknown
28-Mar-98	SA/Roesnes/Johansen	Monteverde/King
2-May-98	SW/Dallin/Woodward	Topham/Twigg/Waterman
27-Jun-98	SA	SA
4-Jul-98	SAW	SA
18-Jul-98	Calloway/Calloway	SA (Re-release)
26-Dec-98	SAW	Topham/Twigg/Waterman
25-Dec-99	SAW	Topham/Twigg/Waterman
10-Apr-99	SAW	Topham/Twigg/Waterman
4-Sep-99	SAW	Topham/Twigg/Waterman
6-Nov-99	SA/Crosby	SA
22-Jan-2000	SA/Crosby	SA
6-May-2000	SA/Crosby	SA
8-Jul-2000	SA/Crosby	SA
5-Aug-2000	SA/Crosby	SA
17-Feb-01	SA/Crosby	SA
6-Oct-01	SAW	Padley/Godfrey
2002	Gamble/Huff	SA
22-Jun-03	Stock/Various	Stock/Crosby/Rass
12-Oct-03	Stock/Crosby/Patmore	Stock/Crosby
21-Dec-03	Stock/Crosby/Patmore	Stock/Crosby
29-Feb-04	SAW/Summer	Riffs & Rays

ACKNOWLEDGEMENTS

I wanted to try and set the record straight without too much vitriol. The Hit Factory was always a team effort, despite what others may have said. There's only so much credit one can give or take before you exceed 100 per cent.

I could not have dedicated my life to the cause without the support and cover of Bobbie. To her should go the accolades. It is due to Bobbie, that our children, Matthew, James and Amy don't look back at those hectic times and feel that they missed a father. I was always there in spirit, if not body. For me, music was a calling, I had no choice – that's my excuse, and I'm sticking to it! Thank you, Bobbie, for sticking with me.

I also want to acknowledge the help and support of Lucy over the past 20 years. Without her I would truly be in a mucking fuddle.

I appreciate the efforts of Jo Hemmings and Kate Michell at New Holland, and those of Chris Welch, who had the unenviable task of transcribing my ramblings and assembling them into something approaching good order.

I have been blessed (or cursed) with undaunted self-belief. I knew at the age of seven, or thereabouts, that I wanted to be a songwriter. The fact that it took me until I was 32 to have my first hit is testament not only to that self-belief but also to the maxim that one should never give up. This, above all, is the advice I should like to pass on.

My greatest regret is that my father never survived to see any of my success. He would have been so proud.

Mike Stock, 2004